A Pestilence on Pennsylvania Avenue

A Pestilence on Pennsylvania Avenue

The Impact of Disease Upon the American Presidency

David R. Petriello

AMERICAN HISTORY PRESS
STAUNTON VIRGINIA

AHP

American History Press

Staunton, Virginia

(888) 521-1789

Visit us on the Internet at:

www.Americanhistorypress.com

First Printing September 2016

Library of Congress Cataloging-in-Publication Data

Names: Petriello, David, author.
Title: A pestilence on Pennsylvania Avenue : the impact of disease upon the American presidency / David R. Petriello.
Description: Staunton Virginia : American History Press, 2016. | Includes bibliographical references and index.
Identifiers: LCCN 2016039285 | ISBN 9781939995179 (pbk. : alk. paper)
Subjects: LCSH: Presidents--United States--Health. | Presidents--United States--History.
Classification: LCC E176.1 .P494 2016 | DDC 973.09/9--dc23 LC record available at https://lccn.loc.gov/2016039285

Manufactured in the United States of America on Acid-free paper
This book exceeds all ANSO standards for archival quality.

To Dr. Richard Petriello, who first taught me to look for where science and history collide, and to my Guinevere, who is the inspiration for everything that I do

TABLE OF CONTENTS

PREFACE

Hippocrates once stated, "It is more important to know what sort of person has a disease than to know what sort of disease a person has." With the amount of influence that age, health, lifestyle, and the indomitable human spirit can have upon illness, this quote is surprisingly accurate and timeless. Indeed, stress from environmental causes or lifestyle can invite illness, magnify it, and complicate its aftermath. While this is true of all people and patients, with the amount of strain that is on those in a position of leadership, either of companies or nations, a study of the impact of disease upon these leaders is both telling and useful.

Studies have been undertaken and numerous books have been written about the impact of religion, war, politics, family, socio-economics, and even height and horoscope signs on the administrations of the various United States presidents, but what of disease? Have the various illnesses that struck the men who led the country, either before or during their time in office, affected their performance or even decision to run? Taken a step further, has the health of the commander-in-chief changed the course of American history?

Disease by itself has affected wars, the economy, demographics, and most notably the exploration and conquest of the New World. Yet, this book in no way seeks to connect every minor virus experienced by a president with a monumental occurrence in the nation's past. Nor is disease in any way the sine qua non of causes in American history. Rather it simply presents an interesting and often understudied addition to an already crowded field of study.

In researching for this work I have attempted to focus on only the most important of presidents and historical events. This book is not simply an encyclopedia of illnesses; it rather seeks to connect diseases to events and then analyze their impact. To round out these connections more fully, chapters have been composed on illnesses affecting various first ladies and first families as well. No president is an island, and the lives of their families certainly played an important part in their evolution as a person and a leader. At the time of this book's publication, Vice President Joseph Biden hedged his entry into the 2016 election, allegedly due in part to the recent passing away of his son, Beau Biden, while Hillary Clinton's own health issues raised concerns among some pundits, and Bernie Sander's and Donald Trump's ages were called into question.

Finally, this topic is timeless. The medical issues which shaped George Washington's presidency or led to the rise of Progressivism also inspired the drafting of the Twenty-fifth Amendment and helped to keep John McCain from the White House. Advances in medicine have not removed illness as a factor in politics, and in many ways may have actually made it more prevalent in political debate. Movement away from the miasma theory has not led, in James Fenimore Cooper's words, "to a people so well fed and so clean." The concept that bacteria and viruses were the carriers for contagion and thus could strike the rich and powerful as well as the common man in the street meant that disease and health should be an important consideration in politics.

A Pestilence on Pennsylvania Avenue

Chapter 1

GELDING THE STALLION OF THE POTOMAC

"I die hard." (George Washington, 1799)

The Constitution did not pretend to be a perfect document, one that addressed every possible problem and development in subsequent American history; much of this would be left up to the various men and women who would hold office in the country. In keeping with this philosophy, George Washington established a number of precedents as the first chief executive of the country, some from choice and some out of necessity. He organized and appointed the first cabinet, developed the idea of executive privilege, delivered the first State of the Union address, and even popularized the term "Mr. President." Less well-known, perhaps, are the many medical firsts that occurred during his time in the military and in office. In fact, Washington's health, or more precisely his occasional lack of it, helped to shape the founding and early development of the nation almost as much as his actions on the battlefield or in the president's chair. The greatest precedent of the first president was the degree to which the health of the man holding the office would impact the entire nation, a factor that would not change for the next 200 years.

General Washington was a rather imposing man, well over six-feet tall, with large hands and feet. One commentator once said of him, "George exuded such masculine power as frightens young women just wakening to the opposite sex."[1] He clearly had a strong constitution as demonstrated by the harsh conditions he endured while on various campaigns throughout most of his adult life. Even after his retirement from office he continued to work actively on his plantation at Mount Vernon. In fact his final illness arose in part due to an hours-long tour of inspection he did around his property in snowy, thirty-degree weather in December 1799.

All of this was in sharp contrast to his immediate ancestors, the majority of whom died young and left fatherless children in their wake. His great-grandfather, John Washington, lived to be 44; his grandfather Lawrence Washington to 39; and his father Augustine Washington to 48. George Washington's own life span of almost 68 years dwarfed those of his forefathers as well as his siblings, who averaged 49 years of life, and showed his strength and vitality.

A number of illnesses befell the first president during his lifetime, and in this he was no different than many other Americans at the time. A brief look at his medical history reveals numerous reoccurring bouts of malaria, diphtheria, smallpox, dysentery, quinsy, and tuberculosis. While participating in the ill-fated expedition of General Edward Braddock towards the Monongahela River, a young Washington was stricken with both hemorrhoids and dysentery, which he referred to as a "pulmonary condition."[2] His letter of several weeks later was less delicate concerning his health: "I was seized with violent Fevers and Pains in my hind which continued without Intermission till the 23 following when I was relieved by the Generals absolutely ordering the Physicians to give me Doctor James' Powder (one of the most excellent medicines in the West) for it gave me immediate ease, and removed my Fevers & other Complaints in 4 Days time."[3] Washington was brought up behind the main army in the back of a wagon. Stricken with illness at the back of the column he was forced to ride into battle on July 9, 1755, with pillows between his bottom and his horse's saddle, a position that helped to save his life once the British regulars marching in the front were ambushed by the French and their Indian allies. In fact Washington's heroic actions at the Battle of the Monongahela, which helped to propel him to national fame, are that much more impressive considering he "was scarcely able to do, as I was not half recovered from a violent illness that confin'd me to my Bed, and a Wagon, for above 10 Days."[4]

One of his childhood illnesses proved to be especially important to the future of the nation that he was to help found. In 1751, a nineteen-year-old Washington traveled with his older brother Lawrence to the Caribbean island of Barbados. The elder Washington had contracted tuberculosis at some time during the previous two years and had visited a number of warm springs and other areas to seek relief for his worsening condition. All of this was quite in keeping with the miasma theory of disease that was popular in that day. Yet, as none of these warm springs seemed to relieve his condition, Lawrence Washington determined to set out for one of the furthest and therefore warmest English ports in the Caribbean—Barbados. As Lawrence's wife had recently given birth to their fourth daughter she was unable to accompany him, so instead he turned to his younger brother for companionship.

George and Lawrence landed in Barbados in November 1751, and the two men remained on the island for only about a month. While Lawrence was not ultimately helped by the climate of the island, the younger Washington ended up suffering the most from the trip. On November 17, he recorded in his journal that he "was strongly attacked with the small pox."[5] The disease ravaged the young Virginian for weeks, leaving a gap in his diary until December 12. He had never experienced the illness as a child and thus had no resistance. Shortly after his recovery the two men returned to Virginia, with the elder Washington dying seven months later, having found no relief for his condition. George was left in charge of Mount Vernon, now a wealthy man at the age of twenty. It was a position inherited by disease that he would work to parlay into political power over the next several years.

The worst was yet to come for George Washington, who contracted tuberculosis himself around this time. While he managed to fight off this contagion as well as numerous other ones, there was a later unforeseen consequence for him. George's marriage to Martha in 1759, though a happy one, was childless. Based upon the four children that she had during seven years of marriage to her first husband, the fertility of the future first lady seems reasonably established. It seems then that the "stallion of the Potomac" was actually a gelding. While many theories have been put forward to explain this, Washington's infertility was most likely caused by the smallpox and/or tuberculosis that he had contracted in his late teens. Numerous studies have shown that both can lead to sterility, especially genitourinary tuberculosis or tuberculosis epididymitis.[6]

The importance to history of Washington's sterility arises from what it possibly prevented. James McHenry once opined to the first president, "You are now a king under a different name."[7] Yet he was far from the only one to make such a statement or take it to its logical conclusion.

In fact, in May 1782 General Lewis Nicola wrote a letter to Washington from Newburgh, New York, that strongly suggested the establishment of a monarchy to be headed by the latter: "This war must have shown to all, but to military men in particular, the weakness of republicks…but if all other things were once adjusted I believe strong argument might be produced for admitting the title of king."[8]

Washington himself was appalled at the notion, writing to Nicola that "No occurrence in the course of the War, has given me more painful sensations than your information of there being such ideas existing in the Army as you have expressed, and I must view with abhorrence, and reprehend with severity….You could not have found a person to whom your schemes are more disagreeable."[9] Yet the thought must have lingered in the minds of some, as one of drafts of the president's First Inaugural Address from early 1789 contained a firm denial on his part of any desire to found a dynasty. Washington went so far as to cite his lack of children as evidence of this.[10] Had a monarchy been established, upon the death of Washington in 1799 a rather messy battle might have commenced between his nephews and his adopted children and grandchildren from Martha Washington.

The simple absence of a monarchy does not prevent the formation of political dynasties. Over the past two hundred years, many states and the nation itself have provided numerous examples of this. One need look no further than the Adams, Harrisons, Roosevelts, Kennedys, Bushes, and Clintons on the national level to be reminded of the frequency and fear of political dynasties. By Washington not having a child he not only prevented the possible formation of a monarchy in his name, but also the more likely creation of a democratic political dynasty.

Washington's own experiences with illness both as a young man and during his time in the French and Indian War led him towards an appreciation of the efforts to curb contagious disease. These beliefs would eventually push him to undertake the largest inoculation campaign in American history up to that time, one that would have a profound effect on the outcome of the Revolution. Smallpox had been a scourge of warfare in the Western Hemisphere since the Spanish conquest of Tenochtitlan in the sixteenth century. Washington's efforts to prevent the outbreak of an epidemic among his soldiers not only decreased unnecessary casualties, but also forestalled the use of biological warfare by the British.[11]

General Washington first became concerned with the issue during the Siege of Boston in late 1775. Rumors began to circulate through the American rank and file that the English besieged in Boston would attempt to introduce the smallpox epidemic then ravaging the city into the surrounding camps of the American rebels by releasing infected prostitutes or runaway slaves into their midst. Four British deserters who appeared in the rebel camp on December 3 confirmed these accounts, which Washington's aide-de-camp, Robert Harrison, reported to the Massachusetts Council in December:

> I am commanded by his Excellency to inform you that four deserters have just arrived at head-quarters, giving an account that several persons are to be sent out of Boston, this evening or to-morrow, that have been lately inoculated with the small-pox, with design, probably, to spread the infection, in order to distress us as much as possible… measures may be taken to frustrate this unheard-of and diabolical scheme.[12]

Not surprisingly, Washington himself was skeptical at first that the British would employ such a tactic, but soon reported to Congress:

> The information I received, that the enemy intended spreading the small-pox amongst us, I could not suppose them capable of. I now must give some credit to it, as it has made its appearance on several of those who last came out of Boston. Every necessary precaution has been taken to prevent its being communicated to this army, and the General Court will take care that it does not spread through the country.[13]

Washington had likewise written to Dr. Joseph Reed:

> The small pox is in every part of Boston- the soldiers there who have never had it, are we are told under inoculation- & consider'd as a security against any attempt of ours. A third ship of people is come out to point Shirley- If we escape the small pox in this camp, & the coun-

try round about, it will be miraculous- every precaution that can be, is taken to guard against this Evil both by the Gen court & myself.[14]

In an ode to medieval warfare, rumors began to circulate that General Howe was to attempt to fire arrows dipped in smallpox pustules into the American camp. While the effectiveness of this method of delivery is questionable, the terror aroused by the idea was real. Fear of contagion being used to sicken him personally even led General Washington to propose dipping all his correspondences in vinegar to sterilize them before handling the letters.[15] Similar worries emerged in Virginia where Lord Dunmore had recruited and inoculated tens of thousands of escaped slaves by exposing them to smallpox, allegedly hoping to send them back to their plantations as Trojan horses of pestilence.[16]

Though he eventually managed to liberate Boston, smallpox followed Washington's army to New York City and on its subsequent retreat to Pennsylvania, claiming more lives than enemy bullets. The respite afforded by the Battle of Trenton allowed him to finally consider the idea of inoculating his men. Writing to Surgeon General Dr. William Shippen he asserted:

Finding the small pox to be spreading much and fearing that no precaution can prevent it from running thro' the whole of our Army, I have determined that the Troops shall be inoculated. This Expedient may be attended with some inconveniences and some disadvantages, but yet I trust, in its consequences will have the most happy effects.

Necessity not only authorizes but seems to require the measure, for should the disorder infect the Army, in the natural way, and rage with its usual Virulence, we should have more to dread from it, than the Sword of the Enemy. Under these Circumstances, I have directed Doctr. Bond [Dr. Nathaniel Bond], to prepare immediately for inoculating this Quarter, keeping the matter as secret as possible, and request, that you will without delay inoculate all the Continental Troops that are in Philadelphia and those that shall come in, as fast as they arrive. You will spare no pains to carry them thro' the disorder with the utmost expedition, and to have them cleansed from the infection when recovered, that they may proceed to Camp, with as little injury as possible, to the Country thro' which they pass. If the business is immediately begun and favoured with common success, I would fain hope they will soon be fit for duty, and that in a short space of time we shall have an Army not subject to this, the greatest of all calamities that can befall it, when taken in the natural way.[17]

Given the prevalent view of most Americans and many colonial governments concerning the operation at the time, Washington's order to forcibly inoculate an entire army was revolutionary. Only sixty years before, Cotton Mather had created a near riot in Boston by lending his support to the practice of variolation, a stance that brought him only contempt and a grenade thrown through his window. Famed patriot Ethan Allen had been put on trial in 1764 for undergoing the same procedure in public. As of 1776, the Council of Safety in Baltimore still forbade the practice among soldiers in order to prevent an epidemic from spreading among the general population. Boston had only lifted its own ban shortly before the signing of the Declaration of Independence, at which time Abigail Adams had herself and her children vaccinated. General Washington had likewise convinced Martha to undergo the procedure in May 1776 in order to protect her should she spend any time with the perennially unhealthy American army.

Opposition was thus both of a religious and practical nature. While Calvinists resented what they saw as attempts to go against the will of God, town elders feared man-made epidemics. Yet Washington understood the dangers of smallpox firsthand. During the French and Indian War, an outbreak of the disease had crippled both the French and their Native allies from 1755 to 1757, and weakened the English forts in New York as well.[18] In fact the war saw ten times as many deaths for the British and Americans from disease as from battle, while 10,000 Acadians died mostly of illness while being forcibly deported from Canada.[19] Dr. Johann David Schoepf, the chief surgeon of the Ansbach Regiment of Hessians, would go on to praise the growing popularity of the practice in America as compared to a continued prejudice against it on the Continent, stating, "The almost universal practice of the innoc of smallpox, whereby countless mult. of children are saved from death, to which the unconq prejudice of our fatherland still continues to offer sacrifice."[20]

To bolster the health of the soldiers further, General Washington and other commanders, most notably Baron von Steuben, issued broadsides calling for a strict adherence to Biblical sanitary codes. These recommendations included the airing out of bedding, the avoidance of sleeping on cold and damp surfaces, the frequent washing or changing of garments (Deuteronomy 23:12), the isolation of sick soldiers (Numbers 5:1-4), and the digging of necessities far from the main camp (Deuteronomy 23:13-14). Washington himself looked towards Moses as the epitome of a successful general who commanded "a great army of the Children of Israel… that continued forty years in their different Camps, under the Guidance and Regulation of the wisest General that ever lived."[21] These moves all shadowed recommendations made by Dr. James Tilton: "Officers therefore, should be very solicitous to protect their men, as well as themselves, from the dreadful effects of filth and nastiness."[22] Overall, Washington's efforts should be credited with not only reducing the impact of disease upon the American army for the remainder of the war, but for helping to popularize the practice of inoculation as the soldiers returned to their various states after the conclusion of hostilities.

Though disease would remain a factor in the war, killing more colonists than did British arms, it did not prevent an American victory. On the contrary, disease in many ways helped to ensure the success of the Revolution.[23] Yet the final victory at Yorktown and the subsequent peace talks at Paris, which served to address the external issues of the new nation, did nothing to resolve many important, internal ones. Chief among these concerns for most was the failure of the Continental Congress to pay properly the many men who had fought or died for independence. Robert Morris, as superintendent of finance for the new country, had enacted a number of strategies to provide for the fiscal stability of the nation and pay those who had served in the military.

Yet as the situation worsened, a troubled Congress announced an audacious plan to pay off the unpaid officers with one lump sum payment. Morris was appalled by the maneuver and resigned in protest in January 1783. With the issue of back pay still unresolved, a meeting of officers was held in Newburgh, New York. Some contemporaries and many later historians labeled the gathering an attempt by the military to launch a coup against Congress in order to seize power. The young American republic, it seemed, was destined to suffer the same fate as the ancient Roman republic. In the end, it was one man and his medical condition which helped to preserve the nascent democracy.

Further adding to speculation as to its goals, the meeting in Newburgh was by invitation only, and was held in a guarded hall. Prominent among those not welcome was their commander-in-chief, Gen. George Washington. Due to his republican views and loyalty to Congress, the conspirators knew they could never fully trust him. Yet it was doubtful that his presence or even the reassurance from Congress that he was to deliver would do much to convince the officers to alter their course of action. What saved the republic from falling in a military coup d'etat was Washington's presbyopia.

General Washington was by this point fifty-one years old and had aged considerably in both appearance and health during the Revolutionary War. He had suffered from presbyopia for a number of years and was forced to wear reading glasses in order to clearly see the frequent letters, orders, and dispatches that he received. However, like many men of his time he was quite vain, and rarely if ever wore the lenses in the company of others. After addressing his gathered comrades and failing to move them, Washington pulled a letter from his pocket from a sympathetic Congressman that he wished to read aloud. Carefully unfolding the document, he strained at first to read the opening line and then paused to pull his reading glasses from his coat and place them on his head. Noticing the puzzled or perhaps even stunned faces of those around him, Washington assured them, "Gentlemen, you will permit me to put on my spectacles, for I have not only grown gray but almost blind in the service of my country."[24] The general's theatrics succeeded, for while the letter from the Congressman was ignored and soon forgotten, his words struck a chord with the gathered officers. Few could disagree that their commander-in-chief had not sacrificed as much or more than those present, and yet asked for nothing in return.

Washington's decisiveness and theatrical flourish arguably helped to prevent a march by the military on Philadelphia and the potential overthrow of Congress. His subsequent pleas to Congress eventually led to substantive relief for the unpaid officers, and his retirement and subsequent establishment of the Order of Cincinnatus helped to prevent the future recurrence of a coup. Though small, further mutinies would arise over the next few years as the issue was slowly resolved, a larger disaster had been averted. Yet the incident, when combined with what was occurring in Massachusetts at the same time, lent further weight to the calls by many for a strong federal government. Both the Newburgh Conspiracy and Shay's Rebellion were catalysts for the Constitutional Convention at Philadelphia.

George Washington had a storied life, filled with battle, achievement, and disease. Over the course of his sixty-seven years, the nation's first president was stricken with numerous illnesses. A brief list of some of the conditions that affected him include three attacks of dysentery, four of malaria, two of tuberculosis, and one each of smallpox and quinsy. Having engaged in constant years of travel and campaigning, it is not at all surprising that the general contracted a variety of illnesses. Yet though Washington eventually settled down to a sedentary life as president, his health problems did not subside.

During his first year in office, the president suffered an outbreak of "a very large and painful tumor," on his left thigh.[25] The most prominent surgeons in New York City, the father and son team of Drs. Samuel and John Bard, diagnosed the ailing leader as suffering from an outbreak of anthrax.[26] The terrible pain caused by the growing lesion kept the president from work and confined him within the official residence on Franklin Square. The busy thoroughfare of Cherry Street in front of the executive mansion was soon closed off to traffic with chains to provide Washington with a level of respite to aid in his recovery. The Bards prescribed surgery as a treatment for the president's condition, with the elder doctor famously advising his son to "cut away, deeper, deeper still, don't be afraid, you see how well he bears it." Because of, or perhaps despite the Bards' treatment, Washington began a very slow and painful recovery over the next six weeks. By September, the president was able to resume most of his functions. The health scare weighed heavily on more than just Washington himself. He stood out as one of the few uniting institutions in a country that had barely approved the adoption of the Constitution, and his death would have plunged the new republic into a crisis. As James Madison himself lamented, "his death at the present moment would have brought on another crisis in our affairs."[27]

Over the course of the next year, the president was stricken with a further series of illnesses. To help aid in his recovery, Washington undertook a succession of recuperative trips, stating, "I have escaped and propose in two or three days to set out for Boston by way of relaxation from business and reestablishment of my health after the long and tedeous complaint with which I have been afflicted, and from which it is not more than ten days I have been recovered, that is since the incision which was made by the Doctors for this imposthume on my thigh has been cured."[28] During this official visit to New England, Washington was detained outside the city of Boston while the town fathers debated the protocol for welcoming a visiting chief of state. Unfortunately the rain and cold bore heavily on the president's weakened constitution, and he soon developed a terrible cold accompanied by inflammation of his eyes. A similar epidemic of respiratory infections was spreading inside the city, which those opposed to the administration quickly dubbed "the Washington Influenza."

Months later, in April, President Washington contracted a severe case of pneumonia, an illness that would again shake the stability of the political system. By mid-May, influenza was ravaging all over Manhattan, with Richard Henry Lee proclaiming the island to be "a perfect hospital—few are well and many very sick."[29] As Washington neared death, the president's handlers and Dr. Bard, snuck Dr. John Jones, the co-founder of New York Hospital and the College of Physicians in Philadelphia, into the executive residence. Once again, to aid in his recovery, the streets around Washington's residence were closed or muffled with straw to reduce ambient noise. Jefferson wrote a series of letters to his daughter detailing every minute of the illness and Washington's eventual recovery. Though the president would improve, the effect upon both him and political watchers was severe. He summed up his illnesses by saying, "I have already within less than a year had two severe attacks, the last worse than the first. A third will put me to sleep with my fathers."[30] In fact, Washington's declining health became a prime motivation behind his refusal to accept a third term in office, thus setting one of the most important precedents in American presidential history.

The president's terms in office also saw the eruption of the Great Yellow Fever Epidemic of 1793, a disease that almost prevented the construction of a new capital in the District of Columbia. Following the outbreak of a bloody revolution on Saint-Domingue in 1791, thousands of French refugees and their slaves had fled north to the United States. By July, thousands had reached Philadelphia and were greeted by a welcoming populace who had even raised $12,000 to help the newest émigrés. Yet, hidden in the hulls of the various hulks that had transported the French to America was another immigrant that had not visited Philadelphia in more than thirty years—the yellow fever virus. Though Dr. Benjamin Rush of Revolutionary fame incorrectly identified the origin of the contagion to be rotting piles of coffee brought in from the Caribbean, perhaps more disastrous was his prescribed combination of bleeding and the ample consumption of mercury to treat the illness.

Conditions worsened with each passing week, and as is customary with such events, various theories and folk remedies arose. Women and boys took to smoking tobacco, as it was thought the smoke would drive away the miasma causing the yellow fever. Some individuals resorted to consuming or wearing garlic, while others avoided barbers and hairdressers, and some began to practice self-bleeding as a means to remove the illness. Pedestrians bypassed sidewalks and used the streets instead, and handshaking become a dangerous rarity. Yet nothing could abate the spreading disease. The local papers reported that the mayor called for the formation of a committee to help the poor and borrowed $1,500 from the Bank of North America for that express purpose. They also carried stories about a local woman who died in the street with her infant still suckling at her breast.

By mid-September, Philadelphia was grinding to a halt. Churches, coffee houses, and the city library had all closed, and three of the four newspapers had stopped printing. Mayor Matthew Clarkson's much celebrated Committee of twenty-six men also faced insurmountable problems when four of its members refused to attend and four died of fever. As the city had replaced New York City as the national capital, the entire federal system began to falter. Though Congress had not been in session since June, the president and many other notables were present during the outbreak. Alexander Hamilton, the secretary of the treasury, was taken ill and soon began to miss cabinet meetings. On September 7 Dr. James Hutchinson, the port physician and an opponent of President Washington, succumbed to the disease. Writing to his secretary of war, the president advised, "I think it would not be prudent either for you or the Clerks in your Office, or the Office itself to be too much exposed to the malignant fever, which by well authenticated report, is spreading through the City; The means to avoid it your own judgment under existing circumstances must dictate."[31]

On September 10, under pressure from his wife and others, President Washington finally decided to abandon the city: "The house in which we lived being, in a manner blocaded, by the disorder and was becoming every day more and more fatal."[32] Withdrawing to General Howe's former Revolutionary headquarters in Germantown, the president queried his cabinet as to his ability to relocate Congress as well. Vice President John Adams was already out of the city, and his official residence of Bush Hill had been turned into a makeshift hospital that soon became "A great human slaughterhouse where numerous victims were inoculated at the altar of riot and intemperance."[33] Many Southern leaders, including both Jefferson and Madison, worried about the effect of the outbreak on the construction of the new national capital along the Potomac River. This move had been an integral part of Southern acceptance of Hamilton's economic plan, but reoccurring malignant fevers could lead to Northern leaders demanding a more temperate location.

Beyond the role of the disease in the debate over the placement of the capital, its treatment became a political issue. Alexander Hamilton and his wife had also abandoned the city as their conditions worsened. Sending their children to Albany, they then withdrew to Fair Hill, some two and one-half miles from the city. Luckily for the Hamiltons, they were soon visited by one of Alexander's boyhood friends from the island of St. Croix—Dr. Edward Stevens. Having a certain amount of experience in dealing with the disease while in the West Indies, Stevens prescribed Peruvian Bark (quinine), aged Madeira, cold baths, and laudanum to help combat the illness. Thanks to Stevens' methods, husband and wife both recovered within five days. Hamilton was so impressed by the doctor's skill that he penned a letter to the College of Physicians in Philadelphia recommending that they follow Stevens' approach to dealing with yellow fever.

Hamilton's letter only worsened the rift between Federalists and Republicans in the city. His rival, Jefferson, went so far as to accuse the secretary of the treasury of faking the illness, proclaiming him as "timid in sickness" as he was in war.[34] Doctor Rush did attempt to recreate Stevens' methods, in a fashion, by throwing buckets of cold water on patients and injecting quinine directly into their bowels, but the results were not promising. The doctor stuck fast to his bleeding techniques, going so far as to blame Hamilton's calls for Stevens' cure, for the deaths of hundreds who possibly would have been saved had they followed Rush's advice instead. Class status seemed to determine treatment, since Federalists tended to follow the advice of Kuhn and Stevens, while Republicans pursued the ideas of Rush.[35]

In the end, perhaps the plague killed 10 percent of Philadelphia's population. Though the economy and the workings of the government did falter, they did not fall. The epidemic nearly led to the removal of the government to the north or further west, moves that would have drastically altered the course of the nation towards civil war. Likewise, it further helped to cement the nascent political parties forming within the young republic.

When George Washington finally left office in March 1797, driven out in part by his declining health, he undoubtedly hoped for many more years of peaceful repose at Mount Vernon. Yet just thirty-three months later he was dead. His retirement was hardly one of rest as he continued to take an active role in the running of Mount Vernon. For about a week in August of 1798, he seems to have contracted malaria and was treated with quinine. Though he recovered, the disease took quite a toll on his health, reducing his weight by almost 20 pounds.[36] A year later, on December 12, 1799, the former president was out riding, inspecting his plantation on a snowy thirty-degree day. It would be hours before he came inside to eat, and when he did so his secretary reported that he refused to remove his wet clothes. By the next day he complained of a sore throat and hoarseness of voice and yet still insisted upon going on his rounds of the property. When he woke at three o'clock the next morning he complained of chills and could barely speak. Home remedies of molasses-vinegar drinks, salve volatile applied to his neck, gargling with vinegar and sage tea, and placing the feet in warm water all produced few positive results.

Doctor James Craik, Washington's physician, applied Spanish fly and bled the president. Soon other doctors arrived, and even though no formal observation of Washington was made, the physicians quickly settled upon removing a quart of blood from him. Dehydration caused the blood to come "slow and thick." Calomel laxative and emetic antimony tartrate administered to the patient further increased his dehydration. In all, over 82 ounces of blood were extracted from Washington, which represented an astonishing 75 percent of the total volume of blood in his body. The former president himself reportedly encouraged the action, stating, "Don't be afraid. The orifice is not large enough. More, more."[37]

Washington's last statement, "I die hard," bore more truth than he might have realized. Between the excessive blood loss and probable mercury poisoning from the calomel laxative, his death was both painful and largely avoidable.[38] The exact condition confronting Washington has been debated in the many years following his death. The two most popular diagnoses remain either acute epiglottitis or quinsy. Either condition, though incurable through bloodletting or the use of mercury, could have been aided through a tracheotomy. In fact the young Dr. Elisha Dick recommended this course of action, but the more experienced physicians present overruled him. He later said, "I know not what might have been the result and it would be presumption to pronounce upon it; but I shall never cease to regret that the operation was not performed."[39] George Washington would expire shortly before midnight, one of the final deaths of the eighteenth century and the second century after the Greek physician Galen.

Yet this was not the end of the man who has often been described as the greatest man of his generation. As the president lay dying, he asked his secretary to "not let my body be put into the Vault in less than three days after I am dead." Numerous contemporary tales existed, no doubt heard by Washington himself, of persons buried prematurely. Three days came and went and the general was laid to rest, no doubt in hope of joining the spirits of his departed comrades. However, not everyone was convinced that he was permanently gone. William Thornton, who was both a physician and the designer of the Capitol building, had been called in to help resuscitate the dying Washington at the end of his illness. Though it seemed to others that he arrived too late to save him, Thornton disagreed. The doctor was convinced that life could be restored to the dead man as:

> The weather was very cold, & he remained in a frozen state, for several Days. I proposed to attempt his restoration, in the following manner. First to thaw him in cold water, then to lay him in blankets, & by degrees & by friction to give him warmth, and to put into activity the minute blood vessels, at the same time to open a passage to the Lungs by the Trachaea, and to inflate them with air, to produce an artificial respiration, and to transfuse blood into him from a lamb. If these means had been resorted to, & had failed all that could be done would have been done.[40]
>
> [Yet]I was not seconded in this proposal; for it was deemed unavailing. I reasoned thus. He died by the loss of blood & the want of air. Restore these with the heat that had subsequently been deducted, and as the organization was in every respect perfect, there was no doubt in my mind that his restoration was possible.[41]

Twenty years before Mary Shelley was to pen her famous work about Frankenstein's monster evoking similar resurrections, Washington was enclosed in a lead coffin and buried at Mount Vernon, as stipulated in his will. The nation would now be forced to survive without him.

Through his illnesses, George Washington affected the birth of the nation to an extent that perhaps equaled his accomplishments on the battlefield. The first president managed to curtail a revolt, forestall a monarchy, popularize vaccination, and establish the notion of a two-term presidency. Likewise the various illnesses that occurred at the time helped to form the party system and even contributed to the American victory in the Revolution. The bar that Washington set for presidential accomplishments was paralleled by his interactions with pestilence, two legacies that would be passed on to future national leaders. Disease could be a positive change agent, causing much advancement as it sowed death and destruction.

Chapter 2

LOBELIA, LEAD, AND THE RISE AND FALL OF OLD HICKORY

"I have to thank my god, my health still enables
me to attend to my duty."
(Andrew Jackson, 1829)

Perhaps George Washington's greatest political contribution to the fledgling nation was his retirement after only eight years in office. His action became the most poignant expression of the American concept of limited government. But term limits and constitutions do not prevent tyranny. Only the virtue of both the leaders and the public ensure the continuation of any republic, and Washington portrayed this quality time and time again. In addition to his concerns over the rise of a tyrant, the first president also feared the birth of political parties, describing in his Farewell Address how ". . . combinations or associations of the above description may now and then answer popular ends, they are likely, in the course of time and things, to become potent engines, by which cunning, ambitious, and unprincipled men will be enabled to subvert the power of the people, and to usurp for themselves the reins of government; destroying afterwards the very engines, which have lifted them to unjust dominion."[42] With the collapse of the Federalist Party not too long after the end of the War of 1812, Washington largely got his wish. Yet a series of diseases was to challenge both views as the nineteenth century progressed.

The end of James Monroe's presidency in 1825 brought about a unique situation in American political history. Due to their opposition to the War of 1812 and suspected disloyalty during the conflict, their gathering of the Hartford Convention, expanding suffrage, and the Republican encroachment into their platform, the Federalist Party was all but dead by 1820. Now, with only one party present in American governance, the office of president stood ready to be passed on, rather than won by contest. A Republican caucus in Congress had chosen William H. Crawford of Georgia to succeed Monroe. Crawford had been secretary of the treasury since 1816 and was popular in many circles, as shown by the fact that he had been the runner-up to Monroe in the caucus before the 1816 election. Senator Samuel Smith of Maryland, in a letter to Jefferson, opined that "Crawford is the best Candidate for that Office, and I shall give him my support. He may at present calculate on N. York [34] or N. Jersey [8]. Delaware [5] Maryland [4] furthermore, Virginia [24], N. Carolina [15] Georgia [9]. Tenesse [3] (at least)—102 Votes."[43]

Some within the party questioned the "democratic" value of selection by Congressional caucus, while others viewed Crawford as a terrible choice for president.[44] This view seems to have been held by the younger generation of the Republican Party. In 1820 Henry Clay, John C. Calhoun, John Quincy Adams, and others had even tried to investigate Crawford's Treasury Department for irregularities in an attempt to smear his name. Yet in the end, the Republican caucus was too powerful for the petty jealousies of a few eager office seekers, and Crawford's nomination and victory seemed all but guaranteed.

This changed dramatically in September 1823, when William Crawford suffered a debilitating stroke. Brought on by the ingestion of a series of prescribed drugs, the proposed future president was temporarily struck blind, deaf, dumb, and paralyzed.[45] Crawford appears to have been suffering from erysipelas, a skin condition caused by streptococcus bacteria, and better known as St. Anthony's Fire.[46] A physician prescribed lobelia, a plant that if consumed in high dosages could cause paralysis, to treat the condition. Crawford was bedridden for eight weeks, and any confidence in his ability to assume the presidency was shattered. An attempt to travel to Monticello to gain Thomas Jefferson's blessing shortly afterwards was derailed by a second illness that only further led people to question his electability.[47]

Prayers and letters of concern from such notables as Jefferson and Monroe began to flow into the candidate's home. On October 17, 1823 James Monroe wrote to James Madison, asking "How is Mr Crawford—and when do you think that he will be able to move? His family, were recovering their health, when I left the city."[48] The true extent of Crawford's illness was elaborately kept secret from almost everyone. Men such as John Quincy Adams simply wrote off the attack as the typical illness occurring at that time of year:

> There has been a very sickly time here these two Months; though not much mortality among persons of your acquaintance—Barron Stackleberg is just getting about, and looks like the Shadow of a Ghost. Mr Bailey is convalescent but not yet out. Madame de Bresson after five weeks of very dangerous illness, is beginning to recover Mr Crawford continues ill at Mr Senator Barbour's in Virginia—Mrs Crawford who has just recovered from illness herself, went yesterday accompanied by Dr. Sim, to join her Husband. He is convalescent, but has been so ill, and recovers so slowly that he will probably not be here for several weeks.[49]

Even without clear knowledge of the true extent of Crawford's condition, it was not long before the political vultures struck. In February 1824, Massachusetts nominated John Quincy Adams to be president, and soon after Pennsylvania chose General Andrew Jackson. Crawford recovered relatively well from his illness, but his opponents seized upon the opportunity to enter the competition for the presidency, especially following Crawford's relapse in March. Both Madison and Jefferson wrote to him following that event, expressing concerns over his recovery, the latter stating, "I enquire always with anxiety of the state of your health, and am concerned to learn that your convalescence is more slow than I had wished and hoped."[50] Crawford largely recovered by the fall of 1824, and men such as Jefferson still predicted his eventual victory in the contest.[51] Though he would live until 1834, he ended up finishing fourth in the November election. The close election was thrown into Congress, where despite Jackson's strong showing in the general election, he was not chosen as the winner. Following the creation of a corrupt bargain, Adams was selected to be the sixth chief executive, with fellow candidate Henry Clay as his secretary of state. The bitterness that would result between Adams and Jackson would tear the political tranquility of the nation apart and give birth to the Second Party System. The nation may have been better served had Crawford's illness or stroke proved to be fatal. His victories in Virginia and Georgia, which were solidly in Jackson territory, may well have gone for the general, paving the way for clear success in the general election. Political parties were reborn in America thanks in part to the misuse of a flower to treat a skin rash.

The next presidential election four years later, which proved to be a rematch between Adams and Jackson, was one of the most contentious in American history. The majority of the issues of the day were thrust aside, replaced instead by personal attacks leveled against both men. Adams was described as corrupt, out of touch, rich, and a pimp for the czar of Russia. For his part, Jackson was labeled an uneducated fool, a murderer, and a man married to a polyandrist. Despite the falsity of the claims against Adams and the veracity of those against Jackson, the latter was elected president in a poignant reversal of the decision of 1824. His inauguration in March 1829 was seen as more than simply the triumph of a wronged politician, but as the victory of the common man over limited suffrage.

Yet the man who was to take the White House was hardly a representative of the young, vibrant spirit of democracy that had propelled him to that position. Though only three months older than John Quincy Adams at the time of his inauguration, he was the oldest president to preside at the White House.[52] Democrats would contend, however, that at sixty-one he was only three years older than the average age of the first six men to hold the office of president. A quick examination of the man's medical background reveals a less than robust figure.

Disease both limited and defined Andrew Jackson. While still a young boy living in the frontier regions during the American Revolution, he had experienced the full depredation of the conflict. After the family was captured and imprisoned by the British at Camden, South Carolina, both he and his brother Robert contracted smallpox in the overcrowded prison camp. Robert died of the disease shortly after their release, while Andrew barely recovered after being forced to walk fever-ridden in the driving rain for more than 40 miles.[53] His other brother Hugh had already succumbed to heatstroke following the Battle of Stono Ferry in 1779, leaving Andrew Jackson the only surviving child. In a final tragedy, Jackson's mother Elizabeth died of pestilence in 1781 in Charleston while attempting to nurse wounded soldiers back to health.[54] Andrew was an orphan by the age of fourteen and held a profound hatred for the British that would later reflect upon his actions in 1818 in Florida with the Arbuthnot and

Ambrister Affair. That incident saw General Jackson invade Spanish Florida in pursuit of hostile natives and subsequently arrest, try, and execute two British citizens without orders from Washington, an affair that almost led to war with both Spain and the United Kingdom. Ironically, much of the confusion that resulted from the invasion of Florida was caused by President Monroe's own serious illness. Confined to his bed, the president was unable to read or approve of the various letters being sent by his commander in the field. Years later, Monroe recalled, "I well remember that...I was sick in bed, and could not read it.... I never read it until after the conclusion of the war." In the end, General Jackson went ahead with the attack by his own accord, severely defeating the local Indians, rising to fame, and causing both a national and international scandal.

Jackson's health problems while in office stemmed from two particular causes. At some point either during his military pursuits in the War of 1812 or the Seminole War, he contracted malaria. Though the disease soon subsided, the lifetime effects plagued him for decades. The Plasmodium vivax strain, which most likely afflicted him, can lie dormant in the liver for years, reemerging periodically to wreak havoc upon its host.[56] Alternatively, Jackson could have contracted the disease numerous times during his campaigns in the southern United States. Either way, the commonly accepted treatment at the time involved bleeding and the taking of calomel, or mercury chloride, and sugar of lead. The toxicity of these cures often proved to be worse than the illness they were addressing. The amount of mercury and lead in the two medicines has historically been connected with the illness and death of such men as Ludwig van Beethoven and Meriwether Lewis.

In addition to the protozoa multiplying within his organs, Jackson permanently held two bullets lodged in his body. Acquired in 1806 and 1813 from duels with Charles Dickinson and the Benton brothers, respectively, the presence of these lead objects certainly helped to elevate the overall amount of the substance in his system. The first bullet became lodged in his left lung, just missing his heart, in part thanks to the large coat he wore which disguised his frame. Wishing to hide the true extent of his injury, Jackson mounted his horse by himself and rode 40 miles to Nashville. The wound was severe, and he spent weeks bedridden and subjected to bleeding. Jackson would report periodic chills, fevers, and chest pains. As a result of this incident, he would cough up blood for the remainder of his life. These symptoms suggest that the future president suffered from an abscess in his lung, clearly a consequence of the duel. Doctors at the time and afterwards often assumed this cycle to be symptomatic of tuberculosis, yet the failure of it to aggravate over time makes this doubtful.

Jackson's second duel occurred only a year before his famed Battle of New Orleans. The bullet lodged near his shoulder, and though his doctors recommended amputation, Jackson refused. Chronic infections would plague him for years until he had the lead slug removed in 1832. While it has been medically argued that his topical use of sugar of lead and his occasional employment of it as an eyewash was most likely not the cause of his subsequent lead poisoning due to its slow rate of absorption, the ever-present bullets certainly could have been.[57]

Between 1824 and 1828, Andrew Jackson lost all of his teeth in rapid succession. This is a classic symptom of prolonged mercury poisoning and most likely arose from an overuse of calomel. Meanwhile, he often complained of intestinal issues, excessive salvation, colic, diarrhea, and tremors. He also exhibited irritability, paranoia, and violent mood swings. All of these could have easily arisen from more than two dozen years of lead poisoning. Some further circumstantial evidence of this is shown by the improvement in the president's health following the removal of one of the bullets from his body in 1832. Afterwards, Jackson wisely turned against the medical use of lead, describing it as "that potent but pernicious remedy to the stomach."[58]

Jackson' illnesses had something of an impact upon his military campaigns as well. During his time spent fighting the Creek tribe in the Deep South, he was stricken with numerous intestinal issues. Despite being confined to bed at the time that he was called into service, Jackson replied, "The health of your general is restored. He will command in person."[59] He liberally employed mercury to help treat his various conditions during the campaign. Jackson's biographer Marquis James famously noted, "Jackson was too sick to leave his bed but strong enough to make war."[60] Likewise, while in New Orleans the next year preparing for his career-altering battle with the British, he was once again stricken with dysentery and so had to issue his early orders from bed. Finally, his tumultuous history with the Territory of Florida was cut short by yet another attack of intestinal inflammation in 1821. In this case it may have simply been a convenient excuse for him to return to Tennessee to begin his political career. This would culminate only six years later with his successful election to the presidency.

Andrew Jackson's health issues bore a unique stamp on his presidency and on subsequent events in American history. Never before had the public or his fellow politicians taken into account the age or health of a candidate. Yet with Jackson's aging constitution, political discourse shifted from talk regarding his mental qualifications to his physical ones instead. Concerns over his advanced age upon taking office were in no way allayed by the numerous bouts of illness that he had faced during his lifetime. At the same time, his arrival in Washington came upon the heels of his wife's death from a heart attack, a death that he blamed solely upon Adams and the National Republicans. When combined with his age and medical issues, the psychological strain of his wife's demise helped to heavily restrict his first year in office.

The president's letters at the time are full of references to his ill health. One of the first was penned only a few weeks after his inauguration and stated candidly: "My labours have been great, my health is not good, but if my constitution will bear me up for one year I have no fear but I will make such an expose to the nation that will be satisfactory to the people."[61] To the husband of his departed wife's niece and the founder of Memphis, John Christmas McLemore, Jackson confided, "I am not in good health."[62] In a similar vein, a letter from Jackson written only two months later to his brother-in-law John Donelson shared the former's now well-established opinion, "My time cannot be long here on earth."[63] Coincidentally enough, the aged Donelson himself would be the first to die the next year, well before Jackson.

Despite his apparent ill health, President Jackson embarked upon a national tour during the summer of his first year in office, a rather rare event at the time. In fact, out of the first fifteen presidents, only three others besides Jackson embarked on official tours of the nation.[64] The various meetings and engagements associated with this seem to have taken a toll on his fragile constitution. By the middle of August, he unexpectedly cancelled his remaining obligations and set out for Rip Raps, an artificial island adjoining Fort Calhoun in the Hampton Roads estuary of Virginia. The president's frequent visits there would earn it the sobriquet of the Summer White House.[65] Jackson had a modest hut built along the shoreline from which he could watch the passing ships and therapeutically bathe in the seawater, which he described at the time as "the fine air & pleasant bath."[66] This watery retreat would also host future presidents Tyler and Lincoln during their tenures in office.[67] Jackson would continue to use Rip Raps throughout his time in office, often making momentous policy decisions while vacationing for his health on the island. Most notable among these pronouncements was his removal of government deposits from the Second Bank of the United States.[68] The Whig press latched onto both Jackson's relocation from the house of the people to a hardened military fortress as well as to rumors of his declining health.[69] Though his health did recover slightly upon his return, perhaps thanks in part to his ample consumption of duck, veal, turtle soup, and whiskey, by September 21 he complained about his various illnesses in a letter to John Coffee:[70] "I had retired a short time since to Rip Raps, for the benefit of my health, which had become impaired from the weight of my labours, and distress of mind—I returned with much improved health, in an absence of thirteen days, but the accumulated business in my absence has kept me so much confined since my return, that it is beginning to effect my health again."[71] In fact, by September 1829 President Jackson was already discussing his plans for a quiet retirement at The Hermitage outside of Nashville.[72]

The numerous health issues that confronted him early on in his administration did not help his already-infamous choleric mood. Jackson often complained about wheezing, swelling in his legs, headaches, blurred vision, and diarrhea. The sparse evidence available leans towards a number of possible conditions, notably a kidney disorder, perhaps caused by the various toxins then flowing through his system.[73] Jackson's temper especially became an issue during the Eaton Affair as well as his fight against the bank.

Shortly after the start of his second term in office, Jackson embarked upon another grand tour of the nation. This time, fresh from his large political victory, he sought to emulate the New England journey of James Monroe over a decade before. No doubt in Jackson's mind his administration was ushering in a second Era of Good Feelings as well. His tour in the summer of 1833 was quickly interrupted by yet another bout of ill health. En route to the North, the president stopped and consulted Dr. Philip Syng Physick in Philadelphia, a physician and surgeon who had famously helped to battle the great Yellow Fever Epidemic of 1793. Physick proceeded to cup Jackson, but to no avail. This was a process that dated back several thousand years which involved placing heated glasses on a patient's bare skin in order to create suction. The president's condition only worsened, with him reportedly suffering from "infection of the throat, bleeding of the lungs, and severe pain in the back."[74] Despite the application of various cures and attempts to bleed him, the president found no relief. He was forced to stay in bed for days, missing the dry-docking of the USS *Constitution* and delaying his reception of a controversial honorary degree from Harvard.[75] While some of his political enemies, most notably John Quincy Adams, doubted the veracity of claims regarding his illness, the president ultimately decided to cut short his goodwill tour.[76]

Many of the events of the president's political career in fact seem tied in one way or another to illness. At the height of the Maysville Road debate in 1830, Jackson became very sick with what was assumed at the time to be dropsy, but was in actuality it was probably associated with his kidney dysfunction. Vice President Martin Van Buren, who following a meeting about the bill had to help the ailing Jackson up the White House stairs, rose to the occasion and became the driving force behind the veto movement.[77] Two years later during his infamous fight against the Bank of the United States, Jackson was confined to his bed "a spectre in physical appearance," with a serious illness.[78] Though the re-chartering of the Bank passed overwhelmingly in Congress, the president told Van Buren from his bed "the Bank, Mr. Van Buren, is trying to kill me, but I will kill it!"[79] His subsequent veto would have profound effects on subsequent American economic and political history.

Jackson gained some additional notoriety for his seemingly constant appeal that a one-term-limitation amendment be adopted for the presidency. In fact the president broached the issue in six out of his eight State of the Union addresses, arguing that it promoted democracy, removed property restrictions, and eliminated corruption: "I can not but believe that more is lost by the long continuance of men in office than is generally to be gained by their experience."[80] Yet the only point at which the idea seems to have gained traction is when the president himself began to assume more powers for his office and seek reelection. Jackson quietly dropped the notion from his speeches during his last two years in office.

To his many enemies and to some of his supporters as well, Andrew Jackson brought a new and perhaps frightening amount of power to the Executive branch. His unlettered background, appeal to the masses, and sole qualification of "killing 2,500 Englishmen at New Orleans," led early on to fears of mob rule and demagoguery.[81] His often-dictatorial assumptions of power after his successful election only served to reinforce this. Whigs took to referring to him as "King Andrew I," while sitting Supreme Court Justice Joseph Story wrote, "Though we live under the form of a republic we are in fact under the absolute rule of a single man."[82] For some time palpable fears existed that the young republic could fall to tyranny or military dictatorship. No less than twenty-one amendments were proposed in Congress at the time in attempts to lessen the power or restrict the term of the president, undoubtedly influenced by fears of Jackson's continuance in office. His archrival Henry Clay proposed just such an amendment in 1841, and wrote often on the subject, referring to Jackson personally in efforts to support his argument.[83]

It was the very dictatorial nature of Jackson's rule that led to the rise of the next great American political party, the Whigs. Dedicated to many of the same industrial and protectionist policies of the Hamiltonian Federalists, the Whigs were also insistent upon increasing the power of the Legislative branch at the expense of the Executive. Seeing "King Andrew" as the embodiment of the very British monarchism that the Founding Fathers had revolted against, they adopted the name used by both many of the patriot leaders and the English political party opposed to the growth of royal power. The Whigs were more than simply a party of negation; they represented a hope to return to the true republicanism of the Constitution. As one newspaper put it, "A Whig in its pure signification means one who prefers liberty to tyranny."[84]

Whig supporters were in part aided in their mission by the second cholera pandemic of 1828, a scourge which had emerged in India and reached the shores of America by 1832. *Vibrio cholerea* is a bacterium which, though existing outside the human body, thrived in the unsanitary, urban environments concurrent with the Industrial Revolution. Once ingested, the bacteria migrate through the intestines producing copious diarrhea, nausea, and fever. As more and more fluid is expelled, the body's extremities begin to turn blue, and death quickly ensues, usually by cardiac failure. Mortality rates can reach as high as 50 percent with the disease killing an estimated 15 million in India alone from 1817 to 1860.[85]

Brought to the United States onboard the Irish "coffin ships," cholera quickly became a political tool for both conservatives and nativists. Many saw the disease as being an affliction of the poor and the sinful. As one historian stated, "Cholera was a scourge not of mankind, but of the sinner."[86] Because of this, quarantines or restrictions on immigration seemed to be the proper course of action to many. Yet to Democrats, quarantines were viewed as an affront to personal liberty, while politically they could not afford to alienate the Irish. Soon, however, one-third of the residents of New York City had fled to the countryside to avoid the illness. In the South, 4,000 deaths were reported in the port city of New Orleans by October.

Due to the unprecedented nature of the disaster, the Dutch Reformed Synod of New York asked the president for a "general observance of a day of fasting, humiliation, and prayer." Jackson's dismissal of this proposal would set off a firestorm during the fierce election of 1832 between him and Henry Clay. The coming of the plague so soon after the unfolding of the Second Great Awakening, a revival of religious fervor promoted by the preaching of Charles Finney and William Miller, and two years after the publication of the *Book of Mormon*, convinced many Americans of the Biblical nature of the outbreak. The situation was described in a contemporary letter written from New York City:

I think the sickness of the city is rapidly increasing. I presume it is altogether unnecessary for me to give you any account of it, as you have the accounts as correctly as we have. It is, indeed, a very solemn spectacle to see sick person carried through the streets in such vast numbers. Also to see 7 and 8 and sometimes 9 coffins thrown into the poor house hearse at one time to be buried. Last week four persons died in one family on the corner of Grand and Crosby-street, within two days of each other; --three lay a corpse and were buried at the

27

same time. Great fear and much excitement prevail almost amidst all classes of people. The cholera! The cholera! Is the common and almost the only topic of conversation. Oh that his fear might lead the wicked inhabitants of this city to humble and unfeigned repentance, for, and forsaking of, their sins.[87]

Clay and the Whigs jumped on the incident, combining it with the president's dissolution of the Bank of the United States to produce a formidable platform. Though in the end Clay would fall short in his goal, the Whigs had at least carved out a niche for themselves in the political world. Now they would consolidate it for the next generation around opposition to Jackson, support for internal improvements, and support for the religious institutions of the North.[88]

As the election of 1836 approached and the Whigs searched for a viable candidate, serious talk was heard about Jackson attempting to attain yet a third term in office.[89] Former Anti-Masonic presidential candidate and attorney General William Wirt declared, "My opinion is that he may be President for life if he chooses."[90] While even a Democratic newspaper at the time told its readers that should a division emerge during the nominating process, ". . . that body will dissipate it in a few minutes, by the nomination of Andrew Jackson for a third term."[91]

The president's various illnesses conspired against him more than Constitutional concerns did. He was suffering acutely from his lung abscess at the time, resorting to having two quarts of blood drained from him as his coughing became more frequent. When combined with his other ailments, he was finally convinced that he was unfit for the strains of national leadership. The fact that most doctors assumed his condition to be tuberculosis would have perhaps convinced him that he had little earthly time remaining. In the end, much like Thomas Jefferson, Jackson stepped aside due to ill health rather than civic concerns, designating essentially a third-term successor in the person of Van Buren instead.[92] The hero of New Orleans alludes to such in his farewell address, reminding those around him that "My own race is nearly run; advanced age and failing health warn me that before long I must pass beyond the reach of human events and cease to feel the vicissitudes of human affairs."[93] If any of the early leaders of the republic would have violated the unwritten rule established by the tradition of Washington and sought a third term, it would have been Jackson. Thanks to a lung ailment and a host of chronic ailments, an early descent to tyranny was averted.[94]

Ironically Andrew Jackson lived another eight years, staying active in national issues, but generally eschewing calls for a return to power. His health continued to deteriorate, and by 1844 he was blind in one eye and had to have his stomach tapped to remove water that was collecting in his body. He declined during 1845 from a combination of ailments including perhaps amyloidosis, erysipelas, and his festering lung abscess. His actual death, which most likely came from possible renal failure, has also been linked by some to the mercury or lead poisoning that plagued him for years.[95] Andrew Jackson was certainly no Cincinnatus. Instead, much like Gaius Marius, he saw his own rise to power inextricably linked with that of the common man, and much like the seven-time Roman consul and general, he continued in power until finally disease defeated him.[96]

Chapter 3

BACTERIAL ASSASSINATION

"Yes, I shot him, but his doctor killed him."
(Charles Guiteau, 1882)

Though the lives of the presidents have all been methodically studied for even the minutest accomplishments, in the cases of several it is their deaths that were actually more remarkable. The demise of several presidents led to their replacement by men who were either ill-suited to or better prepared for the rigors of political life. The mechanism for presidential succession, though laid out by the Founding Fathers, was like many other things within the Constitution—a process that evolved with use and need. Experience with this issue actually predated the adoption of the Constitution. The position of President of Congress began during the First Continental Congress and continued into the period of the Articles of Confederation. It was held by a number of well-known men, including John Jay and John Hancock. Yet the very first holder of the position, Peyton Randolph of Virginia, was only in power from September to October 1774, at which point illness forced him to step down. Upon his return seven months later, in May 1775, his health continued to deteriorate until he died of apoplexy in October of that year. Likewise, Samuel Huntington, who was president from 1779 to 1781, also became ill and was forced to resign at the height of the Revolutionary War. Unfortunately, no procedure was in place in the early republic to compensate for these losses. This became one of the prime reasons behind the creation of the office of vice president by the Founding Fathers at Philadelphia.[97] While the ascension of a vice president to the highest office in the land is often a troubling event, on several occasions it has dramatically altered the path of American history. Nowhere is this more evident than in the rise to office of John Tyler and Millard Fillmore.

The Death of William Henry Harrison

The administration and excesses of Andrew Jackson breathed new life into the conservative movement in America. As we have seen, fears of a return to the tyranny of imperialist rule and the destruction of the checks and balances inherent in the Constitution led to the formation of the Whig Party in the 1830s. Yet, despite a formidable political machine and gains in the House of Representatives and Senate, the Whigs would not secure control over the Executive and Legislative branches until 1840, nearly a decade after their party's formation. It was only after the Panic of 1837 and the unpopular administration of Martin Van Buren that the Whigs, with William Henry Harrison at their helm, were able to handily defeat the Democrats. Thanks to a populist presidential campaign that involved slogans, music, the liberal distribution of hard cider, and an active propaganda wing, the Whigs were able to secure the presidency. They also secured six Senate and thirty-one House seats as well. Clay and his men had been waiting a generation to pass their much hoped for legislation; they were justifiably excited by this revolution in 1840.

President-elect Harrison, though running as a simple, log cabin-raised man of the people, in clear contrast to the elitist, claret-drinking, gold-carriage-riding Martin Van Buren, was nothing more than a creation of his party. The earlier electoral victories of Andrew Jackson and the advent of mass democracy had proven that in order to win, candidates for national office had to be tailored to exhibit certain desirable traits and attributes. Thus the preferred president would be both a military hero as well as a man-of-the-people; in short, a "Jackson." Despite the success of the Whig Party in portraying General William Henry Harrison as such, he was actually descended from one of the wealthiest families in the country, with his father having been both governor of Virginia and a signer of the Declaration of Independence. Nor was he simply just a military man. Before his days in the army defeating Tecumseh and his brother The Prophet, Harrison had studied medicine at the University of Pennsylvania under the famed Dr. Benjamin Rush.

William Henry Harrison had larger political worries than just an exaggerated portrayal of his background. Concerns about his health prompted Whig newspapers to frequently mention his physical strength when discussing his fitness for the presidency: "Old Tippecanoe's bodily health and activity- Gen. Harrison's habit of industry, early acquired, are still retained. The sun never finds him in bed. His mind is as active as his body. He loses no time, and every hour not employed in the active pursuit of his farm is devoted to his books.[98] Part of this concern may have come from the fact that nine out of Harrison's ten children would die early deaths. Overall the family had an average life expectancy of only thirty-eight years.

At the time of his inauguration, "Granny Harrison" was sixty-eight years old, the most elderly president yet, a record which he would hold until the election of Ronald Reagan a century and one-half later. To both combat Democratic suggestions that his log cabin persona meant he was uneducated, and to calm fears in both parties over his age and allegations of his enfeeblement, the new president delivered a lengthy inaugural address.[99] Though edited down by the famous Whig orator Daniel Webster, it still stretched a record-breaking two hours. The speech was detailed and erudite, a summation of two thousand years of history and the entire Whig philosophy.[100] Unfortunately it also required the aged executive to stand outside in the bitterly cold March weather with no hat, gloves, or overcoat. A *New York Tribune* article published after his death stated that two weeks after his inauguration, ". . . the President, in the course of a long walk before breakfast, was overtaken by a slight shower, and got wet."[101] While neither event directly caused his subsequent illness, they were blamed for such at the time.

A week later the president developed a cold, which quickly grew into pneumonia and pleurisy. Newspapers across the country carried almost daily reports of the progression of his condition. Various methods were tried to treat Harrison, including laxatives, suction, bleeding, leeches, cupping, Virginia snakeweed mixed with petroleum, and a Native American treatment involving the application of live snakes to his chest.[102] All amounted to naught as William Henry Harrison succumbed to right lower lobe pneumonia and septicemia or hepatitis, becoming the first chief executive to die in office.[103]

Though his death was certainly mourned by the nation, to some it simply verified what had been presaged regarding Harrison's age. A panegyric by Ann S. Stephens published in the *New York Evening Express*, and later disseminated through most major newspapers, highlighted the issue in between lines of praise for his military prowess and accomplishments:

> The hero came—a noble good old man
> Strong in the wealth of his high purposes.
> Age sat upon him with a gentle grace. . . .[104]

Likewise, the head of the Whig Party, Henry Clay, opined in a letter several weeks later, saying "I share with you in surprize and regret on the account of the unexpected death of the President. I cannot say that it was altogether unexpected to me; for altho' I did not anticipate it quite so early, I told some of his Cabinet that, unless he changed his habits, he could not live long."[105]

What transformed the situation from a simple inconvenience for the Whigs to an outright disaster was the ascension of the vice president, John Tyler. The Southerner had been picked to balance the ticket with Harrison due both to his home state being Virginia and his relative youth, as he was only fifty-one at the time. Yet Tyler was hardly an ardent Whig. In fact he had been the Democratic president *pro tempore* of the Senate during part of Van Buren's administration. However, having been expelled from his party due to his opposition to Jackson's rule by fiat, Tyler became a perfect balancing element to the Harrison ticket. Though he was still a state's rights conservative at heart and opposed to most of the Whig agenda, it was seen as doubtful that he would play any role in Harrison's administration. In fact several prominent Whigs, including Clay and John Clayton of Delaware, had turned down the position, preferring to stay in Congress instead.[106] Yet some within the nation saw the potential for disaster from the nomination of such an elderly candidate. A Democratic committee in Henrico County, Virginia, had written to Tyler only a month before the election in 1840: "Should General Harrison be elected President almost at the age of three-score and ten years, there is no extravagance in supposing that the four years' term to which he has been pledged by himself and his friends, may be anticipated by the course of nature, and the executive power be thereby devolved on you."[107] The letter then went on to query the official view of Tyler on a number of positions, all of which he tended to answer along the lines of the party's plank.

Following a dignified state funeral for Harrison, the nation's attention quickly turned to John Tyler. Not only were the Whigs unsure of what the former Democrat would do, they were equally unsure of what his exact constitutional role should be. Legal scruples and fears over his beliefs prompted the cabinet to suggest a system of democratic rule in the Executive branch, with the president and each member of the cabinet having one vote. Many took to referring to Tyler as "His Accidency," and letters sent to the White House were addressed, "To the Acting President."

President Tyler was intent upon his own path, his own economic agenda, and his own active foreign policy. While in office he arranged for the final annexation of Texas, settled a boundary dispute with Canada, ended a bloody and destructive war with the Seminole, expanded trade opportunities with China, and helped to secure the Hawaiian Islands for future American interests. Yet it was his constant opposition to the economic policies of the Whig Congress that earned him the enmity of his new party and prevented the reinstatement of the Bank of the United States as well as numerous other Whig projects. In fact the president's veto of the bill to reestablish the Bank on August 16, 1841, led to a march on the White House by Whig legislators. Two days after his veto message was dispatched to the Capitol an angry, drunken mob swarmed the front lawn of the president's mansion, throwing rocks, firing guns, and burning Tyler in effigy. An incident slightly later that involved an attack by a rock-throwing assassin against the president even prompted the expansion of Washington's fledgling police force.

Soon his Whig cabinet abandoned him, and he was summarily expelled from the party. An attempt was even made to impeach him in Congress, led by his fellow Virginian John Minor Botts. The president's image sank so low that an outbreak of influenza in 1843 became known as the *Tyler grippe*.[108] One Northumberland, Pennsylvania newspaper stated, "The prevailing epidemic, the 'Tyler Grippe,' has not neglected us in its visitations, and left us almost as prostrate, physically, as its great namesake is in a political point of view."[109] That year Henry Clay, who was also stricken with the disease, commiserated with a friend who had likewise been afflicted: "I sympathize with you in your suffering under the Tyler Grippe. I too have had it, and I found it as mean & insidious as its detestable name implies."[110] The disease appears to have first gained public attention during the president's tour of New England during the summer of 1843. While in Boston for the unveiling of the monument commemorating the Battle of Bunker Hill, Tyler's attorney general and temporary secretary of state, Hugh S. Legare, died from the contagion.

Yet the damage of the first two years of the Harrison/Tyler presidency was not limited to the person of John Tyler. During the 1842 midterm elections, the Whigs lost several seats in the Senate and their hold on the House in a dramatic forty-seven-seat swing. In fact, by the next election they had lost the Senate as well. The Whigs would not control the presidency again until 1848, and would never again control both houses of Congress, leaving their unfulfilled policies to Republicans of the Gilded Age to enact. Harrison, a lengthy speech, and pneumonia had squandered the chances for the Whigs to effectively transform America and prevent or change what was to follow. Though Tyler hoped for re-nomination in 1844, no one took his chances seriously. Instead, the failures of the Whig government to address the economic and social issues of the period helped to usher in the victory of James K. Polk and the period of Manifest Destiny which came with it.

The Death of Zachary Taylor

Polk's presidency was transformational for the American republic. Thanks to both the Mexican War and the Oregon Treaty the nation now stretched from ocean to ocean, fulfilling in large part the dreams of Manifest Destiny. President Polk would himself not seek reelection, and did not live long enough to see the long-term effects of his actions. Only 103 days after leaving office, on June 15, 1849, Polk succumbed to cholera. He most likely contracted the disease during a goodwill tour of the South, perhaps poetic justice for the war he waged on behalf of the slave powers in their efforts to expand to the west. Yet the popular president did not receive the adulations of large numbers of mourners. Fears of his body spreading cholera, if it were handled or approached, led to his corpse being "hermetically soldered within a copper coffin," and then quickly buried with limited fanfare.[111] Yet through the nation's tremendous lurch forward, Polk's efforts brought not only new opportunities but new challenges. The adoption of the Missouri Compromise in 1820 had created a formulaic understanding between North and South over the admission of future slave states into the nation. Unfortunately, the line drawn across the country at the Thirty-sixth parallel did not take into account the vast new territory of California.

The future of California would most likely have transpired more slowly had it not been for the discovery of gold there in 1847. The subsequent, and perhaps most famous, Gold Rush flooded the region not only with settlers but contagion as well. It is estimated that more than 80,000 Native Americans, perhaps half of the population in the region, died from various diseases within a few years of the '49ers arrival. Of the miners who reached California, between 20 percent and 30 percent would die within a year from illness, with 10,000 dying of scurvy alone.[112] The deaths of the natives would prevent any effective resistance against these sickly and weak miners, and therefore helped to secure the region for the United States.

The successful Gold Rush quickly propelled the territory of California towards statehood. However, its desire to enter the Union as a free state made its admittance a point of controversy between the North and South. The issues of equal representation in the Senate and the enforcement of preexisting fugitive slave laws were again the sticking points. . Various Southern states threatened secession and the old lions of the Missouri Compromise—Henry Clay, John C. Calhoun, and Daniel Webster—again emerged to craft an acceptable compromise. Unfortunately, unlike a generation before, the men could not reach an agreement. While Webster was willing to bend on the issue of slavery, Calhoun stood firmly opposed to what he saw as government encroachment on individual liberties, and Clay's insistence on passing the compromise as an Omnibus Bill proved to be a nonstarter. Finally, President Taylor, though a Southerner, stood opposed to any deal, wishing only to see California and New Mexico admitted as two large free states, and threatened to veto much of the legislation. A newspaper at the time referred to him as the "chief antagonistic, no less by instinct then by position" to the efforts of those who sought to divide the nation on the basis of expanding slavery. As the *New York Daily Tribune* put it, "They dreaded more his personal opposition to their contemplated foray on New Mexico than all the forces which the Government can muster there; they knew that a single Proclamation bearing his signature and denouncing the employment of force against New Mexico by Texas would paralyze their efforts to raise troops throughout the South."[113] Tempers flared, and a Southern convention was called at Nashville to discuss the possibility of secession, a move that Calhoun dutifully supported. By March 1850, Webster confided in a letter that the administration was falling and recommended the dissolution of the cabinet: "Hence I fear, the administration is doomed, & the Whig party doomed with it."[114]

Civil war was averted by a number of concurrent diseases that struck the leadership of America. Both Calhoun and Clay were stricken with tuberculosis, with the former being so sick that his speeches on the subject had to be read by others in Congress, since he was too infirm to attend. Calhoun would die of the malady first, in March, thus removing his objections from the bill, preventing immediate secession, and allowing moderates to seize control of the southern Democratic wing of Congress. Much of this was predicted by observers months before Calhoun's death: "If he were to die at this time, his death would be a blessing to the Union…it is a blessing his voice has not been heard in Congress this session on the Slavery question, for we believe it would only have served to still more distract the minds of our representatives, and strengthen the disunion faction."[115] Clay's inability to push through the bill, when combined with his own enfeebled condition, led to his withdrawal from the Senate in August to be replaced in a power position by Stephen Douglas of Illinois.

Most vital to the movement of the stalled compromise was the July 9, 1850 death of the sitting president, Zachary Taylor. While attending a Fourth of July celebration at the Washington Monument, two years after the laying of the cornerstone, President Taylor consumed cold milk and cherries. Within a few days he was reported to be extremely ill, and his condition dramatically continued to decline as the week wore on. His demise is recorded in a contemporary account: "He called for some refreshments, and ate heartily of cherries and wild berries, which he washed down with copious draughts of iced milk and water. At dinner he applied himself again to the cherries, against the remonstrances of Dr. Weatherspoon, and in an hour was seized by cramps, which soon took the form of violent cholera morbus."[116]

As Taylor's conditioned continued to worsen, Weatherspoon called additional physicians and the president's family to the White House. Messages were sent out almost hourly to inform the public of his health, alternately reporting the onset of typhoid and dysentery. The medical treatment provided to the president had not improved much since the days of Harrison, and included opium, ipecac, calomel, quinine, and bleeding.

By July 9, 1850, the hero of the Battle of Buena Vista and opponent of the Compromise of 1850 was dead. The cause of his death has been variously argued to be cholera or gastroenteritis. A cholera epidemic had been ravaging the nation since 1849, and Taylor, unlike Jackson, had even proclaimed a day of prayer and fasting in August of that year in an attempt to assuage divine aid in the fight against the illness. One religious periodical proclaimed, "At a season when the Providence of God has manifested itself in the visitation of a fearful pestilence which is spreading its ravages throughout the land, it is fitting that a People whose reliance has ever been in His protection should humble themselves before His throne."[117] Some historians have even speculated assassination by poisoning, leading to his body being exhumed and tested for arsenic in 1991. While traces of the substance were found, the amount was not enough to cause death. Others have leaned heavily on the treatment provided by his doctors, arguing that they turned a treatable illness into a deadly condition. Regardless of the exact cause of his demise, his opposition to a compromise out West was buried with him.

The new president, Millard Fillmore, was more amenable to the Compromise, almost entirely due to the view that it would preserve the union.[118] As well, Clay's replacement, Sen. Stephen Douglas, was able to push through the bill as a series of measures, thus piecing together various coalitions to achieve the legislation. Thanks to tuberculosis and acute gastroenteritis, North and South were placated and civil war was diverted, but only for another decade. It is not hyperbole to state that the Compromise of 1850 helped to win the war for the North, since the South would have stood a much better chance of successfully seceding in 1850. Much of the advantages of population, railroad, and industry as well as the fervent abolitionism of the Republican Party emerged only in the latter half of the 1850s. Every year of revolt that was delayed by the passage of the Compromise helped to further increase the North's prospects of victory.

Chapter 4

PRESIDENTIAL COVER-UPS

"Whatever you do, tell the truth."
(Grover Cleveland, 1884)

The idea that the health of the president might impact the well-being of the nation is hardly a new one. Both in a moral and a physical sense, the concept has existed since ancient times and has spanned all major civilizations. King Louis XIV perhaps best expressed it: "L'etat, c'est moi." Even with the abandonment of the notion of the Divine Right of Kings and the renunciation of the Royal Touch, the notion of a decline in the leader's health leading to a correlative fall in the nation's economic or political well-being remained. In fact this idea was understood well enough to lead to a number of health related historical cover-ups, notably the deaths of Qin Shi Huangdi and the legend of El Cid. The rise of the American republic did not end this practice, as will be seen with Chester A. Arthur, Grover Cleveland, and Franklin D. Roosevelt. These men sought to avoid the very issues that came with the illnesses of George Washington, Andrew Jackson, William Henry Harrison, Zachary Taylor and others through a series of elaborate cover-ups.

Chester A. Arthur

The stretch of time from the death of William Henry Harrison to the assassination of James A. Garfield spanned forty years and witnessed the death of four presidents. This represents almost half of the nine men who were elected to the office during these four decades. The seemingly pre-destined deaths of presidents in office provoked a crisis in confidence in the stability of the institution. The results of the rise to power of such vice presidents as John Tyler and Millard Fillmore only further drove this narrative. Perhaps an even more disastrous outcome would be the death of both the president and the vice president. Prior to the adoption of the Twenty-fifth Amendment, had Tyler, Fillmore, or Andrew Johnson died in office, the presidency would have passed to the president *pro tempore* of the Senate. This in fact became a real possibility as President Tyler was almost killed during the USS *Princeton* disaster of 1844, an event which killed both the secretaries of state and the navy. As there was no guarantee that the position would be filled by a man of the same party, concerns over the health of these potential successor-presidents, or "heirs-apparent," as Gouverneur Morris preferred to call them, was perhaps as important as that of the president.[119] As a result, after the assassination of President James Garfield, careful attention was paid to the seemingly weak condition of Chester A. Arthur.

Garfield's successor was a man remembered by historians more for his foppishness than for his administration. Arthur allegedly owned more than eighty pairs of pants and changed them several times a day. A product of the spoils system, a contemporary at the time once said, "He'd never do today what he could put off until tomorrow." Far from naturally lazy, Arthur had been a hardworking man earlier in his career, so it seems more likely that it was a medical development that contributed to the decline in his productivity.

Shortly after a trip to Florida in 1882, Arthur was diagnosed with Bright's Disease. This was a general term in the nineteenth century for nephritis or any of a number of similar disorders of the kidneys. A noted change in his behavior occurred soon after his return to Washington as he became lazy, withdrawn, and easily irritated, a far cry from the formerly jovial Arthur of the Stalwart ticket, a faction of the Republican Party which he had supported. The White House and his physicians quickly covered up the true extent of his illness, not wanting to worry the American people, who had already lost two presidents in less than sixteen years. Stories ranging from malaria to sunstroke to seasickness were often fed to the public to appease both voters and the economy.[120] When his actual illness was mentioned, it was done so in a matter-of-fact way or simply downplayed altogether: "President Arthur is said to be suffering from malaria and kidney troubles, and is threatened with Bright's disease."[121] Never was the fatal nature of his condition made public. As part of his convalescence, Arthur traveled to both Florida, in April 1883, and Yellowstone Park later that same year. While the former expedition only worsened his condition after he contracted malaria, his vacation to Yellowstone made the region quite popular with the American public.[122] The park had been established only a decade before, and Arthur's high profile visit inadvertently helped to advance interest in the national park system.[123] All of this paved the way for Teddy Roosevelt's conservationism two decades later.

Arthur's condition only worsened in late 1883, with symptoms of hypertension and an overall generally declining attitude. Choosing not to run for reelection, Arthur retired at the end of his term in 1885. This decision was certainly influenced by the fact that Bright's Disease was considered to be a fatal diagnosis. True to form, his condition deteriorated further and he passed away from a cerebral hemorrhage a short year after leaving Washington D.C. Though Arthur's ill health was well-known to many members of the public, the careful handling of it began a trend that was to intensify under subsequent administrations. All of this would eventually devolve into outright denials, cover-ups, and obfuscations.

Grover Cleveland

The cover-up of presidential illnesses soon became standard fare for the American government and was arguably perfected under Arthur's successor, Grover Cleveland. Vastly overweight and beset with both a drinking and smoking problem, President Cleveland was far from being the epitome of health. Despite these illnesses of choice, though he had nearly died as a teenager from typhoid fever, he remained largely pestilence-free until elected to the presidency. Shortly after his second inauguration, Cleveland noticed a small bump in his mouth. He initially ignored the issue, but by June the size of the growth had increased substantially. Dr. R. M. O'Reilly, the future surgeon general of the army, examined the president and sent a small piece of the tumor, now the size of a quarter, to the army's chief pathologist, under a pseudonym. The latter diagnosed the growth as possibly malignant, and in accord with Cleveland's doctors recommended removal.

Though the late Gilded Age was an era of foreign peace and domestic tranquility for the nation, the president feared panic on Wall Street and throughout the nation should news of his condition or potential operation become public. Congress was set to convene on August 7, 1893, to debate the repeal of the Sherman Silver Act, and Cleveland's leadership was sorely needed. As a staunch supporter of sound money and the gold standard, he was hoping to put an end to the Long Depression then plaguing America. The ill health or even potential death of the chief executive at this moment due to a risky operation could drive the country deeper into financial panic or kill hopes of any compromise in Congress.

The president decided to have the operation performed secretly onboard the yacht *Oneida*, a vessel belonging to his close friend Commodore Elias C. Benedict. The White House informed the press and public that the president would be steaming up Long Island Sound to his summer home on Cape Cod, during which time the operation would surreptitiously take place. The alibi sounded plausible to the public and to the majority of the government as well, and Secretary of War Daniel S. Lamont was the only cabinet member notified of the true purpose of the president's trip. Newspapers at the time gave no more than a paragraph to Cleveland's voyage. The Indiana State Journal summed it up: "President Cleveland arrived here [Newport, Rhode Island] about 7 o'clock this evening. The *Oneida* anchored in the harbor and no one but the steward has been ashore. Few knew of the president being in this locality. He apparently does not desire any demonstration, hence the anchorage in the out of way place, instead of with other yachts in the inner harbor."[124]

Yet the truth of the voyage was much more complicated than a simple pleasure cruise. After arriving at Newark, New Jersey, by train, Cleveland crossed to Manhattan and made his way to the yacht. A team of doctors and nurses headed by Dr. Joseph D. Bryant of New York and Dr. William W. Keen of Philadelphia, who would perform the surgery, met him aboard. After hiding in the cabin while passing Bellevue Hospital in New York to avoid detection, the surgical unit set to work. The added danger of performing complicated surgery on a moving vessel was not lost upon the men, as Bryant told the captain, "If you hit a rock, hit it good and hard, so that we'll all go to the bottom."[125]

Even without the additional complications associated with the operation, this type of surgery, according to Bryant, resulted in the death of one out of every seven patients.[126] Luckily for Cleveland and the nation, the surgery was a complete success, with the entire affair taking only around ninety minutes. Utilizing nitrous oxide, ether, and both topical and injected cocaine, the doctors removed the tumor, five teeth, and a large part of his upper left jawbone. With great skill and foresight, the entire operation was performed inside of Cleveland's mouth, thus eliminating the need for an external incision or the removal of his well-known moustache.

To further the ruse, Dr. Kasson C. Gibson of New York installed a vulcanized rubber plate over the president's missing palette. This allowed Cleveland to regain his vocal abilities, which had been severely compromised by the operation. Reporters were told that the president had an attack of rheumatism and had a tooth removed, but was otherwise in excellent health. Likewise the various cabinet members and other officials who visited him in July and August were lied to and misled. Cleveland proved on occasion to be the weakest member of the conspiracy, commenting to Attorney General Richard Olney, "My God, Olney, they nearly killed me!"[127]

Yet even with all of these precautions, on August 29 a newspaper in Philadelphia broke the story. Both the White House and friends of the president denied it, once again claiming that Cleveland simply had had bad tooth extracted. Elias Cornelius Benedict, when queried by reporters, responded that, "Too much has been said and printed about this matter... if the same operation that was performed upon President Cleveland had been performed you or me not one word would have been said, written, or printed about....We concluded to have it done aboard the yacht where there was perfect quiet and where there were fresh air and good light in plenty. Rather than sit down in an old dentist's chair in a little office in the town on a hot summer day, the president came aboard my boat, and there's all about that."[128]

Cleveland himself went so far as to discredit the reporter E. J. Edwards with a carefully orchestrated White House smear campaign.[129] A 1975 reexamination of the removed tissue confirmed that the president was suffering from verrucous carcinoma of the hard palate and gingiva, brought about most likely by his use of chewing tobacco and alcohol. Yet the overall operation and subsequent cover-up were a success. Cleveland was back in Washington a few weeks later and by August 28, the House had repealed the Sherman Silver Purchase Act.

Cleveland's daughter, Ruth, herself would go down in American culture, thanks to her own death from disease. Born in 1891 while her father was between his terms in office, she quickly became a darling of the American public. Unfortunately, twelve years later, in 1904, the firstborn child of Grover Cleveland succumbed to a bad bout of dysentery. Seventeen years later, the publicly mourned and still popular first daughter became the namesake for the Curtiss Company's new candy bar, the Baby Ruth, at least according to the official story of the company. While others have claimed a variety of alternative histories for the chocolate confection, the Curtiss Company stands by its initial creation myth almost a century later.

Franklin Delano Roosevelt

Perhaps no president has seen a greater cover-up with regards to his health than Franklin Delano Roosevelt. This deliberate obfuscation simply confined to the time of his presidency; it stretched back to his first serious illness in 1921. In fact, attempts to obscure Roosevelt's true health continued even after his death, with his medical file mysteriously disappearing from a vault in the medical center at Bethesda Medical Hospital. Further details of the true state of his wellbeing have only slowly emerged over the past half-century. What they have revealed is that the most serious cover-up concerning FDR's health was not due to his bout with polio, but rather something else entirely.

The disease most associated with President Roosevelt nowadays is poliomyelitis, an illness that has come to almost define him. In fact, a powerful coalition of special interest groups pushed for the memorial to him constructed near the Washington Tidal Basin years later to depict the leader in his trademark homemade wheelchair. Roosevelt allegedly contracted the disease in 1921 while vacationing at his family's palatial "cottage" on Campobello Island off the coast of New Brunswick, Canada. Seeking to escape from both the Newport Homosexual Sex Scandal of 1919, and his depressing loss as the vice presidential candidate in the 1920 election, Roosevelt had gone to the retreat with his family for some much needed rest.

Shortly after his vacation began, he complained of feeling ill, and confined himself to his bed. Rather than quickly recovering from what Roosevelt assumed to be just a minor cold, his temperature instead spiked and he began to experience numbness followed by paralysis in various parts of his body. "I tried to persuade myself that the trouble with my leg was muscular, that it would disappear as I used it. But presently it refused to work, and then the other collapsed as well."[130] His family and personal physician soon sought out additional opinions, and upon trolling the island coincidentally discovered that Dr. William Keen, the same man who had previously operated on President Cleveland, was also staying on Campobello. Keen's diagnosis and proposed treatment of massages was less than helpful, and the fact that he mailed a bill to the family was seen as rather insulting Meanwhile Roosevelt's condition continued to deteriorate.

Though FDR would eventually recover from the illness, he was thereafter paralyzed from the waist down. While it quickly became apparent to those around him at the time that the cause of his illness was poliomyelitis, some have alternately suggested Guillain-Barre disease or some other syndrome.[131] Regardless of the nature of his condition, the promising young politician rightfully feared for his future. His mediocre career as assistant secretary of the navy, remembered largely by the Newport Sex Scandal, combined with his loss in the election of 1920, had already served to darken his potential for office. Roosevelt certainly feared that the physical and emotional impact of his illness, along with its interpretation by the public, would put the final nail in his political coffin.

Ultimately, rather than accept defeat and a slow decline into mediocrity, Franklin Roosevelt fought back. Years of physical therapy ensued, augmented with the use of appropriate leg braces. In June 1924, only a couple of years after his health-altering illness, Roosevelt was featured prominently at the National Democratic Convention in his home state of New York. Arriving on stage with a pair of crutches, he placed Governor Al Smith's name into nomination with a laudatory speech. Though the Ku Klux Klan wing of the party ultimately crushed the Catholic governor's chances, the address marked the reemergence of Roosevelt on the national stage.

His ascent to the top of the speaker's platform was merely the first in a long line of attempts at disguising his condition that involved both herculean efforts as well as mercurial subterfuge. Thanks to his leg braces and his strengthened upper body, Roosevelt was occasionally able to walk on stage using only a cane. At the same time, most of his speeches saw him gripping a platform, railing, or the arm of his bodyguard or son to give the illusion of standing. This charade of virility was not always successful. On June 27, 1936, Roosevelt was at Franklin Field in Phila-delphia to accept the nomination of his party for the presidency. Before an ecstatic crowd of 100,000 he was driven towards the stage, which he was then helped up onto, his physical movements obscured by the sheer number of luminaries and delegates on the platform. While crossing the stage towards the speaker's podium, he went to shake hands with famed poet Edwin Markham, who suddenly fell into Roosevelt, pushing him to the ground and snapping one of his leg braces. Roosevelt's well-trained security detail quickly sprung into action, fixing the brace and steadied the president before the crowd noticed anything more than a stumble.

Despite more recent historical revisionism, Roosevelt's illness was not unknown to the public or ignored by his enemies at the time. In fact it was made an issue during his first major foray into politics since his loss in the election of 1920. Roosevelt opted to run for governor of New York in 1928, being chosen by the Democrats to succeed his old friend Al Smith, who was then busy running for the presidency. Republican periodicals questioned FDR's ability to handle the physical demands of the office. In response, Al Smith opined, ". . . but the answer to that is that a governor does not have to be an acrobat. We do not elect him for his ability to do a double back-flip or a handspring. The work of the governorship is brain work. Ninety-five percent of it is accomplished sitting at a desk."[132] The disappearance of Roosevelt's paralysis as an issue probably had more to do with his opponent's fears that it would garner sympathy votes for him than any attempt by the Democrats to cover it up. At the same time Roosevelt did his best to de-emphasize his illness as well. During his term in office in Albany, the press was discouraged from taking any photos that would reveal his condition. The governor himself once quipped to re-porters, ". . . no movies of me getting out of the machine, boys."[133]

The presidential election of 1932 once again brought the issue to the fore. This time though it was the Democratic Party that struck first, launching an alleged attack piece by self-proclaimed Republican writer Colonel Reginald Earle Looker, in actuality a pre-emptive strike to discredit Roosevelt's health as an issue.[134] The medium they chose was *Liberty* magazine, a periodical that reached over two and one-half million people at the time, making it the second most read magazine in the nation. An article published in July 1931, a full year before the Democratic convention, alerted readers, "It is an amazing possibility that the next President of the United States may be a cripple."[135] The candidate's entire medical history was then laid before the American public, acknowledging his bout with infantile paralysis and his reliance upon a cane and even including a picture of his leg braces. Interestingly though, any reference to his use of a wheelchair for conveyance was tactfully omitted. Looker couched his story and demands for a medical investigation of the future candidate in sound history, pointing out the near calamities caused by the medical states of both Warren G. Harding and Woodrow Wilson only a little more than a decade before.

The article in *Liberty* then skillfully attempted to portray the governor's weakness as an actual strength. When questioned by the author, Roosevelt admitted that he did not, "move about my office," but added that this allowed him to concentrate more on his work. Photos were also included showing the future president swimming at Warm Springs, Georgia, which he said helped to restore the feeling in his legs. Nowhere in the article was his near total paralysis admitted in any detail. His wife Eleanor was also included in the piece, attempting to calm readers by humorously stating, "If the paralysis couldn't kill him, the presidency won't."

Looker concluded that FDR ". . . seemed able to take more punishment than many men ten years younger." The various medical men the author interviewed likewise agreed. The magazine commentary was a successful coup by Roosevelt's election team, who afterwards sent copies to every corner of the nation. A similar story appeared that same year in *Time* on February 1, 1932. Much like the expose in *Liberty*, this one emphasized the positive elements of Roosevelt's ailment. The story though was then taken to the level of pure fantasy when it stated that "Governor Roosevelt is confident of ultimate total recovery."[136] While some magazine articles written both before and after his election did mention his use of a wheelchair, there seemed to be little concern among the public.

Overall, though Roosevelt's health was certainly an early topic during the election cycle in 1932, it hardly received the microscopic inspection that it would today. This is most likely due to the combination of a number of factors. Most important of these was the extent of the economic disaster that was then overshadowing the nation. The majority of the public cared more for answers to their personal financial issues than for rumors about the president's health. Second, the Roosevelt faction successfully disarmed the concept prior to the main campaign against the Republicans. Finally, the public at the time had more personal experience with the disease and may not have concerned themselves with it as much as the modern observer might do.

That is not to say that during his time in office, President Roosevelt and his administration did not endeavor to cover up his lameness. The Secret Service became somewhat notorious for assaulting photographers who attempted to snap a picture of the president in his wheelchair, by seizing their cameras and exposing their film.[138] In fact the only obvious attempts to highlight Roosevelt's disability seem to have come from adversarial sources. *Life* magazine printed a picture of the president in a wheelchair in 1937, much to the consternation of the White House. This was not surprising, since Henry Luce, the owner of the periodical, was an ardent Roosevelt opponent.

Beyond the subterfuge of the Roosevelt White House with regards to the president's illness, some historians have attempted to examine the policy impact of his polio. A 2005 biographical film on the subject, *FDR: A Presidency Revealed*, portrayed the New Deal as an attempt by the paralyzed Roosevelt to project strength, a classic psychological paradigm. A *Washington Post* article written in review of the movie stated, "Because voters were unaware of Roosevelt's paralysis, he set out to project a can-do approach calculated to restore national self-confidence."[139] As part of this, the president became the face of the March of Dimes, an organization which he helped to found in 1938 to combat infantile paralysis. Thanks to its efforts and funding, in 1954 Dr. Jonas Salk created a vaccine to defeat the disabling disease.

Historically speaking though, the preoccupation with his polio by both the White House and the American public distracts from the larger medical cover-up of the administration. The president's overall health began to deteriorate slowly during his second term in office. While it is not unusual for a president to suffer increased physical ailments due to the weighty demands of his position, Roosevelt's own battles with heart disease and other issues were not only unprecedented, but were covered up in a dramatic bid to secure his hold on power during World War II. Interestingly enough, his co-conspirator was Dr. Ross T. McIntire, the personal physician to the president and a student of Rear Admiral Cary Grayson, the man who had helped orchestrate the cover-up of President Wilson's illness twenty years before.

Despite the disappearance of Roosevelt's personal medical file, it is possible to piece together his slow and steady decline in health. It seems that as early as 1937, the president was beginning to suffer from heart disease. He was first reported to have systolic hypertension in that year, followed by diastolic hypertension in 1941. His condition seems to have worsened by January 1944, at which point he complained of headaches, shortness of breath, and blacking out events. McIntire called in Dr. Howard Bruenn of Bethesda Naval Hospital, who immediately diagnosed the condition as hypertensive heart disease and recommended digitalis. His advice was ignored for almost three months, during which time pulmonary edema set in. This tell-tale sign of congestive heart failure finally prompted McIntire to give the president digitalis, a procedure that would continue almost up until Roosevelt's death. His diet was thereafter closely monitored and his intake of cigarettes was cut from an alleged twenty to thirty per day to around five to six.[140]

Congestive heart failure was not the only life-threatening condition from which the president suffered. According to a number of recent studies on the subject, it appears that Roosevelt may have been suffering from cancer as well. Medical as well as pictorial evidence exists for the possibility that the president had at least one bout with melanoma. Photographs from the 1930s onwards show an enlarged, pigmented lesion above his left eye. Later photographs from his third term show the lesion to be missing, and in its place a scar. This in itself would not have been odd had it not been for a number of other associated health events.

In 1941, the president is reported to have suffered from a bizarre episode. While the White House officially documented the story as a case of bleeding hemorrhoids, the shear amount of blood Roosevelt lost seems to push for an alternate diagnosis. It was reported that from May to June of that year, the president lost two-thirds of the blood in his body. This would be a shocking case of hemorrhoids, but not out of the ordinary for a lower gastrointestinal bleed from a tumor. Roosevelt underwent nine transfusions before being cleared by his doctors. A similar operation was performed in 1941 for Harry Hopkins, one of the president's closest advisors, who was dying from stomach cancer.

FDR's condition seems to have only worsened as time progressed. In late November 1943, while he was attending the Tehran Conference, Roosevelt suddenly became ill at dinner and had to be wheeled out of the dining hall. One witness stated that "Roosevelt was about to say something, when suddenly, in the flick of an eye, he turned green and great drops of sweat began to bead off his face."[141] Rumors had been spread by the Soviets of an impending German assassination plot and some American delegation members were fearful. Back in Roosevelt's room Dr. McIntire performed a quick examination and determined the president to be merely the victim of indigestion. After returning home, he spent the month recovering from what the press dubbed the "Tehran Flu." Not everyone was in agreement with the diagnosis. Dr. Harry S. Goldsmith would later suggest that this episode marked the beginning of Roosevelt's heart failure or worse yet, a spreading tumor.[142]

Further stomach ailments arose in 1944 when on April 28 the president suffered an acute abdominal attack while vacationing at the home of Bernard Baruch in South Carolina. McIntire diagnosed it as a case of acute cholecystitis, or an inflammation of the gallbladder. Roosevelt was treated with injections of codeine for the next week, and until May 4 he experienced cycles of pain. By the end of the month, he was back in the capital for a cholecystogram, the results of which allegedly showed some buildup of cholesterol, but otherwise a healthy gallbladder. A number of conditions could have resulted in this condition, including a tumor. A further abdominal attack would occur during the summer, this time as he sat talking to his son James.

The cover-up of Roosevelt's true condition began early on in his third term. Dr. McIntire would submit samples to various hospitals and noted medical men under a variety of pseudonyms, some as basic as F. David Rolph. As the election of 1944 approached, these efforts were increased to the point of actively misleading the American public. The famed Boston surgeon, Dr. Frank Lahey, who specialized in colon and stomach issues, was consulted. He advised the president not to run due to his heart disease. A recently released letter from Lahey, held in secret for years, made clear his professional opposition to a fourth term for Roosevelt: "As a result of activities in his trip to Russia he had been in a state which was, if not in heart failure, at least on the verge of it…over the four years of another term…be unable to complete it."[143] Bruenn put FDR on a low fiber diet in the summer of 1944 following his gallbladder attacks. The president's weight quickly began to fall, reaching 188 pounds by June and 165 pounds by November. McIntire became concerned at this rapid weight loss and ended the diet regimen, adding daily dosages of eggnog to Roosevelt's meal plan to help him maintain his weight. Around the same time, his doctors reduced his working day to only four hours. In a letter, Roosevelt confided to Churchill that he worked little more than three days a week. At such a critical juncture in the war this is especially striking.[144]

The cover-up late in the election cycle of 1944 may have actually hastened his demise. In August the president made a trip to Puget Sound Naval Base in Bremerton, Washington. While delivering an address aboard the USS *Cummings*, FDR was suddenly overcome with sharp chest pains. In order to further help dispel rumors about his weakness, Roosevelt had agreed to deliver his entire speech standing, supporting his weight only with the podium. While he may have been able to perform this feat a decade prior, his advanced age, declining health and recent weight loss made this an untenable act. In fact his drastic decline in weight caused his leg braces to no longer fit properly, thus placing additional strain on his arms and chest. After a half hour of speaking he suddenly began to experience sub-sternal pain. His physicians feared a myocardial infarction and ordered an EKG. Opinions are still split as to whether the president may have suffered an angina or simply muscle strain in his chest and back. Either way the episode further demonstrated his lack of physical ability to carry on his position.

A similar attempt to convey the image of a robust Roosevelt occurred later in the fall. His staff insisted on driving him in an open-air car in the autumn rain through the streets of New York City. However, this effort at portraying vigor was both ill advised and counterproductive. The president had to be carried from the vehicle, and rubbed down by his aides in order to ensure warmth and feelings in his limbs. By the time of the election, his mouth sagged and his shirt necks were too loose. FDR was far from the image of health and ability that he had been in 1932.

Well before other presidents used the IRS or FBI to secure their position in power, the Roosevelt White House employed J. Edgar Hoover's organization to investigate any potential leaks regarding the president's health. A letter from Hoover to Stephen T. Early, the president's press secretary, describes one of these investigations:

> It seems that Dr. —— is a Lieutenant in the Navy, assigned to the Bethesda Naval Medical Center and residing at ——. When interviewed on October 27 relative to any statement which had been made concerning the state of the President's health, Dr. —— denied making any statements of this kind, but stated that the President's health had been the subject of a general discussion at a luncheon recently held at the Naval Hospital in Bethesda. When asked to name specifically the persons who had attended the luncheon, Dr. —— declined to do so and stated that the reason the President's health had been discussed at the hospital was because members of the hospital staff recognized the picture of one of the Navy Hospital doctors, Dr. H. G. Bruenn on the President's train at the time he was making the acceptance speech. Dr. —— stated that he had not discussed the subject of the President's health with Dr. Bruenn. Dr. —— was obviously disturbed and uneasy during the interview.[145]

Despite the campaign of misinformation waged against the American people, Roosevelt and his inner circle were under no misapprehension as to the president's fate. Even Dr. Lahey himself, in a confidential and conscience-clearing letter, advised that if FDR ". . . does accept another term, he had a very serious responsibility concerning who is the Vice President."[146] The man currently holding that office, Henry Wallace, was objectionable to conservatives within the Democratic Party. His past issues with mysticism, his flirtations with socialism, and his month-long odyssey through Siberia, where he viewed and praised the Stalin's gulags, failed to inspire confidence in the public. Though many considered the "assistant president," James F. Byrnes to be the logical choice, the president was concerned with his conservatism, anti-labor views, and past Catholicism. Roosevelt forwarded two names to the Democratic convention in July for consideration, Senator Harry S. Truman and Associate Justice William O. Douglas. The former was seen as the better choice due to his Southern appeal and less scandalous personal life. Douglas supporters later claimed that his name had been first on Roosevelt's note, but that Chairman Robert Hannegan had reversed the order before delivering it to the gathered delegates.[147]

The president's last year in office was spent readying for both the end of the war and the end of his life. He made sure to invite all thirteen of his grandchildren to what he knew would be his last inauguration, an event which was held at the White House rather than at the Capitol. Though the official story for this much smaller event was ". . . the war was on and the President's time was occupied," his declining health was the more appropriate reason.[148] At the same time he began to lay plans for his own funeral, while naming his son James his executor. A visibly infirm Roosevelt also attended the infamous Yalta Conference in February 1945. His daughter Anna, who served as his advisor and caregiver, accompanied him. There has been much historical debate as to what part his declining mental and physical health played in the unwise concessions that he granted to Stalin. This is particularly true with regards to China, when after only a thirty-minute meeting Stalin was granted control over Mongolia and much of Manchuria. Interestingly, Roosevelt was not the only dying member of the delegation. The ever-infirm Harry Hopkins had to disembark at Algiers due to his illnesses, and the president's close advisor Edwin "Pa" Watson died of a stroke on the voyage home.

Roosevelt's health declined sharply after his return from Yalta. As Patrick Hurley, the American ambassador to China at the time, would write five years later in an article for *Atlantic Monthly*, Roosevelt was "a very sick man at Yalta."[149] Many would comment on the president's apparent lack of mental focus, his sagging face, and his generally cadaver-like appearance. In April he began to complain of "a terrific pain in the back of my head" while at Warm Springs, Georgia, with his longtime mistress, Lucy Mercer Rutherford. This discomfort was a brain hemorrhage, which would ultimately kill him on April 12, 1945, a short three weeks from the end of the war in Europe and Hitler's own demise. The exact cause of the hemorrhage and whether it was connected to his heart disease, or possibly cancer, remains open to debate. Much like Abraham Lincoln, Roosevelt would not live long enough to see the results of his labors or aspirations while in office.

Despite the official presidential line, as can be seen by the brief sketch of his health above, Roosevelt had actually been the sick man of Yalta and the dying man in the White House for some time. His heart disease and probable cancer certainly made him unable to function to the degree necessary for those weighty issues that occurred during his last year in office. According to Dr. Louis E. Schmidt, a close friend of Anna Roosevelt:

For several years before his death he had a lot of 'little hemorrhages,' small blood vessels bursting in his brain. When these burstings occurred—and they were frequent during his last years—he would be unconscious (completely out) although sitting up and apparently functioning for periods of from a few seconds to several minutes... these were occurring regularly at the time he was meeting with Churchill and Stalin and holding other momentous conferences of the utmost importance to the United States.[150]

These "little hemorrhages," which most likely were transient ischemic attacks, were clearly warning signs of a more serious health issue. From this we are left to assume that much of the president's third term was compromised, as was his fourth, a chronology that would encompass much of America's time fighting in World War II. This disclosure shines a new and perhaps uncomfortable light on many of the major episodes of the war, including the various conferences, the invasions of Italy and Normandy, and the domestic aspects of the conflict as well. All of this was kept from the American people in a cover-up undoubtedly deemed necessary for the war, but the question of whether the nation would have been better served by a physically or mentally healthier leader during its last few years remains striking and unanswered.

Interestingly enough, the cover-up of Roosevelt's health continues unabated more than seventy years after his death. The construction of an appropriate monument for him in Washington not only involved a debate over whether to portray him in his wheelchair, but also expunged his other trademark item, his ever-present cigarette holder. This sanitization of the president's image is merely a modern extension of what he himself did in the past. In the end the same question of motive arises, are these moves for the benefit of the people or the man himself?

Chapter 5

THE FIRST FEMALE PRESIDENT

"Please open the window, please, I smell death in here."
(Katherine Anne Porter, in *Pale Horse, Pale Rider*)

The impact of Franklin Delano Roosevelt's illness upon both his presidency and subsequent American history pales in comparison to the changes wrought by the sicknesses of Woodrow Wilson. In fact the two men share much in common, not just in terms of politics and the vast struggles that they faced abroad, but with their poor constitutions as well. Each was sickly upon assuming power and both experienced subsequent steady declines in their mental and physical abilities. Worse though were the effects that their conditions had upon the nation and the extent to which they went in order to deceive the American people.

Woodrow Wilson never had the striking figure or larger-than-life presence of some of his predecessors, men such as Theodore Roosevelt or Andrew Jackson. He was instead an academician, and visually fit the mold with both his thin frame and pince-nez glasses. Despite playing baseball and being an avid sportsman, both his mental and physical health were somewhat frail. Beginning early in life he often experienced stomach problems, no doubt exacerbated by his fat and grease heavy Southern diet.[151] From at least the 1890s until well into his presidency, Wilson would utilize a stomach pump to remove what he considered to be the bad acids from his stomach. At the same time he would swallow small amounts of charcoal to line and calm his digestive system.[152] The procedure was antiquated and in fact potentially dangerous. Once when performing it, Wilson broke the pump off in his esophagus after having pumped his stomach full of water to clean it out. He was quickly rushed to the doctor to embarrassingly have his stomach drained.[153] Wilson continued to use this procedure to self-treat his stomach ailments during a good portion of his presidency.

The larger issue for President Wilson however, and the one which was to have a lasting impact on the nation, was his heart disease and the associated strokes that accompanied it. Wilson seems to have suffered from atherosclerosis throughout much of his adult life. Besides the speculative evidence of this condition associated with his stokes, some secondary indications exist, among them his diet and photographs of his face during his time in office. The few pictures that exist of a smiling Wilson show him to have had terrible dental health. As is now well-established, periodontal disease can be linked to atherosclerosis. President Wilson would have had a number of risk factors for heart disease.[154]

Though Wilson wrote of a "temporary illness" that affected his nerves in 1891, he seems to have suffered his first major medical episode in May 1896.[155] Having purchased a new property at the recently-renamed Princeton University, Wilson was giving extra lectures and working countless hours to earn enough money to pay for the renovation of his domicile. At the end of the term, he was suddenly struck with a weakness in his upper right arm and was unable to use his fingers on that hand. It would take months for him to be able to write with his right hand again. His doctors diagnosed his condition as either writer's cramp or neuritis, simple inflammation of the nerves.[156] Wilson went so far as to consult Dr. William Keen, the same physician who once operated on Grover Cleveland and who would also misdiagnose Franklin Roosevelt. In the meantime his wife sent him to England for a two-month summer vacation, during which time he relaxed and gradually regained his health. This was to be the first of many mysterious attacks on Wilson's health.

During Wilson's nine-year tenure as the president of Princeton University, he suffered no less than five other noteworthy attacks. Again almost all of these were isolated to his right arm, some were associated with rather stressful events in his life, and all took months to recover from. His first episode in his new position occurred in June of 1904 while he was working hard to revise the curriculum of the university and it once again resulted in an immediate weakness in his right arm. Though he recovered physically from this attack much more quickly than he did in 1896, he seems to have suffered some long-term mental or emotional trauma, performing several unusual acts in the weeks following his stroke.[157] One of the more notorious involved his dismissal of a beloved professor, while shortly afterwards a protest broke out after Wilson's construction of a fence around Prospect House. Much of this probably resulted from a combination of his academician view of the superiority of mind over body as well as his Calvinistic outlook of his illnesses as a personal rebuke from God.

A second attack happened only two years later. Once again Wilson was heavily engaged in his work as president of Princeton, this time proposing the controversial quad plan to reorganize campus life on a more democratic basis. Much of the faculty and student body were split upon the proposal, leading to several contentious meetings and protests. Though the plan was eventually defeated, the larger loss was Wilson's own health. During the night of May 27-28, 1906, he lost vision in his left eye due to a retinal hemorrhage. The most likely cause of this condition was a blockage in the central retinal vein in the eye, yet another effect of his hypertension. His vision would be permanently damaged from this attack, with him having only limited peripheral sight from his left eye. At the height of the debate on the subject of the quad plan in November 1907, he seems to have had another attack, reporting numbness in his right fingers, a condition which seems to have lasted for several more months.

Several minor attacks occurred between 1908 and 1910 while the future president continued his reorganization attempts at Princeton. In July 1908, he seems to have suffered two additional bouts of "neuritis," once again confined to his right arm. These followed closely upon a heated student presentation in the spring at the annual *Princetonian* dinner, once again against the proposed quad system. Finally, in December 1910, he reported weakness in his perennially affected right hand. This episode came closely upon the heels of his election to office as governor of New Jersey, a position he would hold until March 1913. Interestingly enough, Wilson reported no further medical issues during his time in Trenton, despite a rather ambitious Progressive agenda while in power.

Wilson would attempt several cures and treatments for his perennial strokes during this time. Perhaps the most bizarre was his correspondence with the renowned Physical Culture charlatan Alois P. Swoboda. An Austrian immigrant, Swoboda had made a name for himself purporting to be able to cure most illnesses and even repair damaged organs. Wilson wrote to him in 1901, and upon his advice began to drink four pints of water a day to increase his blood supply.[158] Though the consumption of at least eight cups of water a day is recommended as healthy by most modern day institutions, this would hardly have helped to correct his atherosclerosis or prevent future strokes.

Once again, save for the weight of Taft, health was not made an issue during the election of 1912, much to the benefit of the Democratic Party. Woodrow Wilson's election to the presidency in November 1912 would be the height of both his short political career and the nadir of his personal health. Several small episodes of numbness in his extremities served as a warning sign of a future impending medical issue. The first occurred only a month after his inauguration in March 1913, and was once again localized in his upper right arm. Two years later he lost much of the feeling in his right hand, a condition that was to last from May to September 1915. In August 1915, the president seems to have suffered another medical emergency, this time affecting his right eye. Wilson's personal physician, Dr. Cary Grayson, recorded the incident in a letter to his wife:

> My number one patient in this house had an accident last night with one of his eyes—the good one, which is bad now. I am hurrying off to Philadelphia with him at six o'clock tomorrow morning to consult an eye specialist. We are going by motor. I think we can make the trip less noticeable in this way…The papers will read something like this: The President made his annual visit to the oculist etc etc.[159]

True to form, most major papers reported this cover story faithfully.[160]

Grayson had been the naval physician aboard the presidential yacht for both Franklin Roosevelt and William Howard Taft, and now had risen to the rank of rear admiral and the position of White House physician. He became a trusted advisor to the president as well, and was well-positioned to formulate the cover-up that was to ensue regarding Wilson's ability to hold office. Grayson's letter to his wife quoted above was merely one example of the cloak of secrecy that he would weave while in the White House. He carefully controlled the president's diet and workload in an effort to keep him healthy enough to remain in office. While Wilson worked a rather sparse day upon taking office, this was subsequently reduced upon the advice of Grayson and others to a mere three to four hours a day by the time of his reelection in 1916.[161]

Wilson's health continued to deteriorate despite the best efforts of his physician. From 1915 to 1919, he complained of a constant onslaught of severe headaches, some of which would keep him from work for hours or days. Many of these were explained away as the result of stress, various illnesses, or even from the occasional overindulgence in wine, yet they were most likely the sign of a deeper problem.

Wilson's re-election campaign in 1916 played out in much the same way as Roosevelt's had in 1940. Both were sick men who probably should not have been their party's standard bearers. But personal conviction combined with looming war threats to prompt both men to run. Woodrow Wilson ran on an anti-war platform, which was the popular view among most Americans after watching World War I produce a bloody stalemate in Europe for more than two years. No evidence exists to posit how Wilson himself felt about his health in 1916, but there exists plenty of proof as to what he felt of the uniqueness of the times. Under pressure from his closest advisors, Wilson agreed to a plan, should he lose the election, of convincing Vice President Thomas R. Marshall and Secretary of State Robert Lansing to resign, replacing the latter with his opponent, Charles Evans Hughes. The president would then himself step down from office immediately as "times are too critical to have an interim of four months between the election and the inauguration of the next President."[162] Though in the end the Republican candidate could not defeat Wilson, the latter's health certainly did.

During the summer of 1918, as the war in Europe was beginning to shine more favorably upon the Allies, President Wilson underwent a secret surgery. Dr. Grayson remains one of the few sources on this procedure, telling his wife, "The patient is progressing most satisfactorily, so far, and I have good reasons to hope for a most beneficial result. It has been a big undertaking.... No one knows anything about it except Miss E., Miss Harkins, Hoover—It is one secret that has been kept quiet, so far, and I think it is safe all right now."[163] The secret operation was ostensibly to correct a breathing problem that Wilson was suffering from, possibly polyps in his nose. Whether it is connected to his later, more deadly illness is unclear and perhaps unimportant, but it does further illustrate the deceptive nature of the White House when it came to Wilson's health.

The more drastic turns in his well-being took place in 1919, after the arrival of President Wilson in Paris for the Versailles Peace Conference. Though he had failed to take any major Republicans with him, the president did travel with one of his most trusted confidants, Dr. Grayson. For four months Woodrow Wilson negotiated and fought with both England's Prime Minister David Lloyd George and Prime Minister Georges Clemenceau of France. Though he had arrived in France preaching the Fourteen Points and promising no harsh punishments for the Central Powers, the Allied leaders stood in the way of Wilson's idealistic dreams. After months at an impasse, Wilson threatened to return home to America rather than compromise on his plans. In the evening of April 3 this abruptly changed. President Wilson suddenly became violently ill, with a high fever, coughing, and diarrhea and was confined to his bed. The suddenness and violence of the attack led some of his closest associates to assume that he and his immediate delegation had been poisoned. In fact one of the president's aides who was similarly ill would die only four days later.

Wilson had most likely fallen victim to the Spanish Influenza pandemic, or some other serious strain of the virus, which was then ravaging the entire planet. Over the course of only a few months in 1918 and 1919, more than 50 million people on the planet would die of contagion, with perhaps a third of the world's population infected. Though the disease would disappear as quickly as it had arrived, it would send more people to the grave in a short amount of time than any other illness in history or World War I.

The Spanish Influenza struck the world in a series of three waves. The first outbreak of the flu occurred in March 1918 in Kansas. A group of men from Haskell County, Kansas, who had signed up for the armed forces was reporting to Fort Riley for basic training. Eighteen of the recruits were reported to the Public Health Service as sick with symptoms of influenza when they arrived at the fort. By the second week in March, the fort reported more than 500 cases of the disease. Soldiers brought it to Europe with them, and outbreaks were reported there by May. Due to wartime censorship, few reports of the actual extent of the illness showed up in newspapers. Only from Spain, which was neutral during the conflict, did stories emerge of the true horrors of the epidemic. An estimated 80 percent of the population of that nation contracted the illness, including King Alfonso XIII. The lack of censorship in Spain and frequent stories of the king's illness and recovery led to many believing the disease had originated there.

Though Dr. Grayson was quick to deny that the president was stricken with the deadly illness, the press quickly seized upon the story and openly questioned the effect that it would have on negotiations.[164] Reports that famed surgeon Dr. J. Chalmers Da Costa was being rushed to Paris on a "routine assignment," only elicited more speculation.[165] In the midst of his bout with the deadly pestilence, Wilson called upon Lloyd George and Clemenceau to meet with him to continue talks. Various aides and political officers noticed a marked change in the president. He was quick to anger, forgetful, delirious, and unable to think in the sharp manner in which he could before the attack.[166] Lloyd George himself recorded Wilson's "nervous and spiritual breakdown in the middle of the Conference."[167] Some of his decisions and comments were erratic and even verged on insanity. The president suddenly forbade American diplomats from using automobiles to get around Paris, began to bury important papers in the yard, and demanded that furniture be assigned to the different nations based upon race.[168]

The president's psychosis drifted into the negotiating room as well. Numerous members of the American delegation resigned in protest as the president suddenly began to give in to French, Japanese, and Italian demands. The harsh punishments demanded by Clemenceau imposed upon Germany, thanks in part to Wilson's sudden change of heart, would help to directly lead to World War II. In a final tragic episode, in June 1919 a note arrived from a young Vietnamese petitioner named Nguyen Ai Quoc, one of the founders of the French Communist Party. The letter was couched in the very ideals of Wilson's own Fourteen Points and demanded independence for the people of Southeast Asia. Existing records show that the letter was received by the American delegation, though it is impossible to judge if Wilson himself ever read it. Regardless, the demands went unheeded and produced only further bitterness and disillusion among the Vietnamese residing in Paris. Young Nguyen Ai Quoc especially did not forget the hypocrisy of the United States, a lesson he would carry with him even as he changed careers, countries of residence, and even his name. It was after his last change that Americans would best remember Nguyen, who eventually rechristened himself Ho Chi Minh, the communist leader of North Vietnam.

Wilson's supporters and later apologists were quick to argue that though the president had not achieved complete success, his death at the time would have resulted in a worse treaty. According to Wilson's private physician, Cary T. Grayson:

> The president was suddenly taken violently sick with the influenza at a time when the whole of civilization seemed to be in the balance. And without him and his guidance Europe would certainly have turned to Bolshevism and anarchy. From your side of the water you can not realize on what thin ice European civilization has been skating. I just wish you could spend a day with me behind the scenes here. Someday perhaps I may be able to tell the world what a close call we had.[169]

Wilson's bout with influenza may have drastically altered the Versailles Conference, but a further illness upon his return home doomed any chance of America participating in his one victory. Out of the many points that Wilson hoped to achieve in the aftermath of the Great War, his most treasured was the League of Nations. Even if he compromised on every other issue, the League, once in existence, could correct these problems. Therefore it became imperative for the United States to ratify the Treaty of Versailles and join the League, and it was incumbent upon the president to convince the citizens and congressmen of this need.

Wilson's attempts to ensure the election of a larger Democratic majority to Congress in 1918 failed spectacularly as the Republicans swept into power. Likewise the president's insistence on bringing only loyal supporters with him to Versailles only further hardened the views of the opposition against him. Thus in 1919 Woodrow Wilson decided to utilize Theodore Roosevelt's old weapon of the bully pulpit and undertake a speaking tour of the nation.

Beginning on September 3, 1919, President Wilson embarked by rail on a trip across the country. He would ultimately cover 8,000 miles in only twenty-two days, a truly grueling pace but one, which showed the seriousness of the situation. Unfortunately the trip began to wear upon his health and he was soon complaining of headaches and shortness of breath. By the time he reached the Dakotas, he was reported to be rambling and discussed more domestic issues than the actual concept of the League.[170] Though he improved slightly upon reaching the West Coast, he experienced a full mental breakdown after his train departed from Pueblo, Colorado. After examining his patient, Dr. Grayson ordered a halt to the speaking tour and had the train take Wilson directly to Wichita, Kansas. Despite protests from the president, his campaign to convince the nation to join the League was over.

Wilson's headaches continued on the train ride back to Washington, growing worse as the days wore on. Soon his vision began to fail, and by September 25 he was reporting weakness on the left side of his body. Less than a week later, on October 2, his wife found him prone and bleeding on the floor of his bathroom in the White House. Edith Wilson instantly called for Dr. Grayson, who examined the president and pronounced him to be the victim of a stroke. Despite his near total helplessness and paralysis, however, a movement was quickly undertaken to secure him in power. Mrs. Wilson and Dr. Grayson organized an unprecedented cover-up with almost no information allowed out to the American public about the president's true condition. In fact though former president Taft would write to a friend only three days after the stroke, "McAdoo says the President is in a state of collapse—that his mind is clear but that he is so weak that his doctors would not permit him to discuss or think about any of these matters.... He says that he would like to help, but he is in a delicate situation, being the son-in-law of the President." It is doubtful whether he knew the full extent of the president's condition.[171] Taft blamed Wilson's campaign for the League as the cause of his apparent breakdown: "He has so insisted on hogging all the authority—trusting no one—that he has broken himself down."[172]

Attempts were made by some to push for the president's immediate resignation. Secretary of State Lansing notified Wilson's private secretary, Joseph P. Tumulty, of his desire to see the president's condition documented and revealed to the public, but the latter refused to certify it. Dr. Grayson not only supported Tumulty's decision, but also threatened Lansing. Perhaps it was a deep seated fear that removing him from office would only kill the man, or an even more apocalyptic notion that his resignation would certainly doom the vote on the Versailles Treaty which had compelled Edith Wilson and Cary Grayson to begin an almost yearlong campaign of obfuscation. Besides the American public, the vice president and much of the cabinet were left in the dark as well. Wilson was kept confined to his bedroom, with Edith serving as the official go-between for the next year and one-half. Though word did begin to leak out almost immediately, the full extent of his illness was unknown. Further complications soon followed, including a urinary blockage and a prostate infection, which only further convinced Grayson and Mrs. Wilson of the need to keep others away from Woodrow. Even an official committee formed by the Senate in November to investigate the true condition of the president reported back that he was of sound mind.[173]

Mrs. Wilson, for all intents and purposes, began a regency that was to last for months. Despite her claim that "I, myself, never made a single decision regarding the disposition of public affairs," this was simply not true.[174] In fact, only three weeks after he was felled by the stroke, Edith approved a veto of the Volstead Act on her husband's behalf, but most likely without his knowledge. Though this was simply a formal veto due the overwhelming support that the act had, it still gave credence to concerns at the time of a "government by petticoat." The first lady saw delegations from both Europe and Congress, including a visit by the Prince of Wales.

Meanwhile debate on the Treaty of Versailles continued unabated in the Senate. Without Wilson's guidance and leadership, supporters of the League began to falter. Henry Cabot Lodge's reservations about the treaty were a serious stumbling block to ratification. By the time Wilson was coherent and cognizant enough to dictate advice to the Democrats in Congress he was a changed man, even more obstinate than before. He urged his devotees in Congress not to accept any compromise, which in effect doomed the League. His condition was not helped by the fact that in January 1920 he once again was stricken with a severe case of influenza followed by another episode a month later. By this point even Grayson talked of resignation as a viable option both to save Wilson and possibly the Treaty.[175] Wilson reacted by lashing out at those around him as much as he did against the irreconcilables in Congress. Perhaps his lowest point came in February 1920, when he fired Secretary of State Lansing, ostensibly for holding cabinet meetings during his period of indisposition.

The final vote on the League came in March 1920, when it went down in flames on the floor of the Senate. The president's own mental health continued to crumble as a result of his strokes and his policy losses. Apocryphal stories arose relating how either he, or by his order the Secret Service, began to roam the streets of Washington arresting speeders.[176] He would even tease his family members and relatives at dinner, asking which of them was stopped for speeding today. On other days he would complain about the condition of the trees in various parks throughout around the capital. Yet despite all of this, Wilson held out hopes of running for a third term in 1920, hoping to once again make the nation's entrance into the League of Nations the central topic of the election. Wilson even went so far as to help scuttle the candidacy of his own son-in-law and secretary of the treasury, William McAdoo, in order to push the party to nominate him instead. His goal seems to have been to secure a vote on the League after his victory and then quickly resign from the presidency.[177] Overall he feared that by not running he would be turning over control of the party to the William Jennings Bryan wing of the Democrats, men who supported isolationism. Contrary to his own optimism, others did not share his hopes for a nomination. Representative Benjamin G. Humphreys II, a Democrat from Mississippi, even took to the House floor in 1920 to demand that Wilson publicly disavow rumors that he was seeking a third term. Once again, much as with Jefferson and Jackson, a combination of his ill health combined with the precedent set by Washington prevented the Democratic Party from even considering this as an option.[178]

In the end Wilson faded out of his presidency. The Red Summer of 1919 and the revitalizing election of 1920 distracted Americans from their perennially ailing leader. The United States would never join the League of Nations, effectively crippling that organization and leading to its ultimate demise. Between the president's bout of influenza and his stroke, the path had been laid out for a slow march toward World War II. Wilson's health, or lack thereof, was perhaps one of the most pivotal political illnesses of the twentieth century, shaping world events for a century.

Chapter 6

AN ACCESSORY
TO
ASSASSINATION

"I deny the killing, if your honor please. We admit the
shooting." (Charles Guiteau, 1881)

Though American presidential history is replete with talented doctors,
from the medical skill of Benjamin Rush to the ingenious cover-ups
performed by Cary T. Grayson and Ross McIntire, not every president
was so fortunate in his choice of physicians. Washington's previously-de-
scribed relationship with his own doctors and surgeons at the end of his
life clearly helped to hasten his demise, a trend that would be repeated
numerous times over the next two centuries. Despite advances in medicine following the death of the first president, medical mistakes by White
House physicians would continue unabated until almost the present day.
Some of the more serious errors by presidential doctors may have even
altered the fate of the nation.

James A. Garfield

James A. Garfield had been elected president in 1880 by fewer than 2,000
votes on a platform of civil service reform, an issue that had grown pressing since the implementation of the spoils system by Andrew Jackson fifty
years prior. Debate over the danger of patronage was still unsettled when
only four months into his tenure Garfield was shot by "disgruntled office
seeker" Charles Guiteau. Though the latter was clearly insane, his status as
a product of the patronage system gave much impetus to Garfield's cause
in the immediate aftermath of his demise.

Guiteau had stalked the president for days, waiting for the perfect opportunity to strike. The president's wife, Lucretia Rudolph Garfield, had been suffering from malaria since May 1881 with a fever of 104 degrees, and the couple had decided to travel to the resort town of Elberon, New Jersey, to aid in her recovery.[179] Due to the malarial nature of the environs of the White House and the presence of open sewage around it, both Garfield and the press had recommended that the first couple distance themselves from the building. "Mrs. Garfield is too ill to be moved, or she would be carried to some healthier place than the White House at once."[180] Because of the seriousness of her condition, their departure to New Jersey ended up being delayed by almost a month. Guiteau had planned to kill the president on June 18 as he departed from the Washington train depot, but lost his courage when he saw the poor condition of Mrs. Garfield.[181] Two weeks later, as the Great Comet of 1881 streaked overhead, the president walked arm-in-arm with Secretary of State James H. Blaine into the Baltimore and Potomac train station for yet another trip. He entered the ladies waiting room to wait for his locomotive when Guiteau succeeded in his mission. Two bullets from the assassin's .442 Webley Bulldog hit the president, with one injuring his arm and the other entering through Garfield's anterior thorax and lodging itself near his pancreas. The president miraculously survived the assassination attempt and was carried back to the White House. Defying the views of his doctors, Garfield's condition even seemed to improve over the next few days. This respite was not to last, however, since the unsanitary probing of his wound by doctors spread infection throughout his body. Alexander Graham Bell was even summoned to the White House to design a primitive metal detector in hopes of finding the exact location of the bullet, but unfortunately the metal bed frame that the president lay upon rendered his invention useless.[182]

Garfield's condition worsened and he soon lost over 70 pounds, reducing in weight to little more than 130 pounds by August. His doctors even resorted to the extreme measure of feeding him rectally for more than six weeks in order to build up his strength.[183] Yet as his condition only worsened, the president was moved to the Jersey Shore to aid in his recovery. Navy engineers even created an early version of air conditioning, positioning fans over a giant block of ice in order to cool down Garfield.

Unfortunately none of these innovations helped the ailing chief executive, and eighty days after he was shot, Garfield died in mid-September. At his trial, Charles Guiteau argued that he was innocent since his bullet did not actually kill the president. Though he was not believed at the time, post-death autopsies and more recent science have proven him right.

President Garfield actually died from a combination of causes brought on more by his own personal health and the medical malpractice of his doctors than from Guiteau's bullets. The various physicians working on the president had probed his wound using only their unclean fingers. Worse yet, they had misjudged the path of the bullet, in effect creating an additional channel in his body, enlarging his wound and allowing in deadly bacteria. The pus draining out of Garfield towards the end of his life was a sure sign of widespread septicemia. Pneumonia soon set in as well, and Garfield, who was already suffering from ischemic heart disease, died due to an aggravated heart attack. In a similar vein to the demise of Washington almost a century before, Garfield had been killed by his doctors.

There was much debate at the time over this very premise. In late October, only a month after Garfield's death, Dr. Robert A. Gunn publicly stated that the president's wound was not fatal and that it was the actions of his physicians that had ended his life. Gunn specifically blamed the constant twisting of Garfield's body to change his bandages, the use of morphine, and most damaging, the feeding of the president by enema. "One of the greatest fallacies the profession has ever advocated. Dozens of patients have been killed by this method of feeding."[184]

Regardless of the causes of his death, Garfield's demise helped to usher Chester A. Arthur into the White House. The importance to American history of this "ascension by assassination" was that even though Arthur himself was a Stalwart and a product of the spoils system, popular outcry now called for a reform of the structure. Continued public concern even cost the Republican Party seats in Congress in 1882. In response, the Pendleton Act was passed through bipartisan effort and signed into law by Arthur in January 1883. In effect, civil service reform had been brought about thanks to the medical malpractice of Garfield's doctors.

Additionally, the death of Garfield led to the removal of his ailing Secretary of the Navy William H. Hunt. Hunt had pushed for more Congressional funding for the shockingly dilapidated navy. In the end he only attained approval for the construction of two vessels, but no actually funding for doing so. Arthur replaced Hunt with William E. Chandler, a much more accomplished bureaucrat who a newspaper at the time referred to as "regarded with some dread by the barnacles, torpedoes, and rats. . . . He will soon reorganize the Navy Department with a very stiff broom."[185] Thanks to Chandler's efforts Congress finally approved and funded the construction of four new steel ships—the *Atlanta, Boston, Chicago,* and *Dolphin.* The commissioning of these warships represented the birth of the modern American navy.[186]

William McKinley

Only twenty years after the assassination of President James A. Garfield, another violent attack felled President William McKinley. While it seemed to many Americans that ever since the death of Lincoln, tragedy was visiting the chief executives of the nation every generation, the fault again lay more in the health of the presidents and their choice of physicians than the actions of their assassins.

William McKinley was at the height of his presidency and popularity in 1901. His list of accomplishments in four short years dwarfed many of his immediate predecessors, including placing the nation firmly on the gold standard, ending the Long Depression of 1873 to 1896, acquiring Hawaii, Puerto Rico, and Guam, and winning the Spanish-American War and liberating Cuba. His re-election, though marred by the ongoing Philippine Insurrection, was hardly a closely contested affair. Once safely back in the White House, McKinley resolved to revisit the issue of the tariff that he raised only a few years before in a bid to extricate the nation from the Depression. With prosperity returned to America, he now hoped to pursue a series of reciprocal trade agreements with various European nations.

President McKinley set out on a nationwide tour in 1901 to present his ideas to the American public. His original itinerary called for him to travel the length of the country, eventually ending in Buffalo in the middle of September on what had been coined "Presidents' Day." Joining him on this journey, beyond the usual collection of government officials and trusted advisors, was his beloved wife, Ida McKinley. The first lady had a history of poor health and is believed to have suffered from seizures. William McKinley seemed the epitome of chivalry in the care he afforded his often-ailing wife, allegedly throwing a handkerchief over her face at dinner parties whenever she suffered a seizure.

A few weeks into the trip, Ida McKinley fell ill and the migrating White House was quickly pushed along to San Francisco ahead of schedule. Newspapers reported that her case involved simply a felon on her finger, most likely caused by the large amount of handshaking that she had been doing. McKinley's doctor lanced the swelling twice, and by May 14, 1901 she was reported to be steadily improving. Yet barely twenty-four hours later rumors spread that she had taken a turn for the worse. The remaining tour was quickly cancelled and a deathwatch was instead set up. Newspaper headlines on the May 16 reported that she had only hours to live, with dysentery having set in.[187] Though she did ultimately recover, a distraught McKinley would postpone the journey to Buffalo until September.

At the same time that the president and first lady were being hurried back to the capital, another equally distraught citizen was likewise making his way slowly to Buffalo and destiny. Leon Czolgosz was an unemployed twenty-eight-year-old who had lived most of his life in Detroit. After losing his job in 1893 at one of the lower points of the Long Depression, Czolgosz had turned towards anarchism for answers. After meeting personally with Emma Goldman in Cleveland in May 1901 the young anarchist thought that the appropriate response to the condition that both he and so many other workers were experiencing was to kill the president.

By September 4, 1901, both men were in Buffalo at the Pan-American Exposition. Czolgosz had arrived the day before and had already purchased a .32 revolver at a local hardware store. As the president and his party were disembarking from the train, a poorly orchestrated cannon salute shattered the windows of the depot. Many onlookers dove to the ground or fled, thinking that an anarchist bombing had taken place. Incidentally Czolgosz was in the crowd, but could not get close enough to the president to assassinate him.

The president frequently clashed with his advisors when it came to the matter of his personal security. McKinley loved to meet and welcome his well-wishers and in so-doing made himself an easy target. The anarchist once again attempted to shoot the president, this time on September 5, as the latter gave a speech out in the open in front of a crowd. Much like the first attempt, Czolgosz was jostled too much by those around him and could not get a clean shot.

McKinley's fateful moment came the next day as he welcomed visitors to the Temple of Music, one of the main attractions at the Exposition. The president was said to be quite adept at shaking up to fifty hands a minute, gently swinging each well-wisher past him in order to keep the line moving. Towards the end of the event, Leon Czolgosz approached, his right hand wrapped in a bandage. As McKinley grasped at the assassin's left hand, Czolgosz shot him twice in the abdomen with the gun that he had concealed in his wrapped up palm. "I did my duty," screamed the anarchist as nearby men leapt onto him while others caught and comforted the mortally-wounded president.[188]

The first bullet was reported to have struck him in the chest, but was deflected by either his breastbone or a button and was found in his clothing a little later. An attempt was made to contact famed local surgeon Dr. Roswell Park, but he was at that moment in the middle of a very delicate operation in Niagara and refused to come until much later. In the meantime Dr. Herman Mynter began treating the president with both strychnine and morphine, while Dr. Matthew D. Mann, a gynecologist, administered ether in preparation for an examination to find the remaining bullet.

The medical room at the Exposition was far from ideal for such a delicate operation. There was little light now that night was approaching, despite Thomas Edison's rigging of the entire fair in electric light bulbs, and little to no useful medical equipment. In addition, McKinley's obese frame made it difficult for his surgeons to probe effectively for the bullet. Much like with Garfield a generation before, the doctors relied upon inserting their fingers into his body in order to do so. Two holes were soon discovered in the president's stomach, both of which were quickly sutured with black, silk thread. The medical team speculated that the bullet must have lodged somewhere in McKinley's back, but unable to find it they simply closed up his wounds and hoped for the best. No apparent attempt was made to actually clean his wounds, nor was an X-Ray machine put to use, although one was sitting nearby as one of the highlights of the exhibit. Both professionals and the public questioned this decision almost immediately: "Nine out of ten people believe the surgeons should have used the X-ray in President McKinley's case."[189] Contrary to popular opinion, the machine was not an unknown mystery to the public at the time. In fact McKinley himself had viewed an X-ray image of a leg shattered by a cannonball from a Civil War veteran applying for a position as postmaster.[190] After finishing an operation on another patient in Buffalo, Dr. Park arrived at the Exposition, but did not interfere with the two doctors out of professional courtesy.

McKinley survived the impromptu operation, and frequent updates of his condition were wired across the nation and throughout the world. Though at first he seemed to be improving, this was merely superficial since gangrene was slowly spreading from his stomach to his pancreas and kidneys. The government took extreme measures to save the chief executive. In fact, only a day after the shooting Thomas Edison dispatched an X-ray machine with a team of operators at the request of McKinley's personal secretary George B. Cortelyou. Likewise his doctors began to feed him by enema in order to ascertain the strength of his digestive system. While the former attempt proved to be as much of a failure as Alexander Bell's machine twenty years earlier, McKinley's body was able to hold down the food that was given to him, a reassuring sign to those who were following his condition.

Yet only two days after his first successful oral intake of food he collapsed. Unable to hold on any longer, President McKinley died in the early hours of September 14, 1901. The autopsy that followed revealed a much more complete picture of what had befallen the president. The bullet that entered him tore through his stomach and transverse colon, nicked a corner of a kidney, passed through his peritoneum, and caused damage to his adrenal glands and pancreas. Despite a four-hour exam, the bullet was never found. It was discovered that the president suffered from cardiomyopathy, which would have severely diminished his chances of recovering from the gunshot, the subsequent botched surgery, or the resultant infection. The generally accepted cause of death today is pancreatic necrosis resulting from the damage done to the organ. The failure of McKinley's doctors to find the bullet, clean the wound, and employ an X-ray machine properly, when combined with his preexisting heart condition, led to his subsequent death.

The immediate aftermath of the assassination included numerous patriotic marches, as well as physical assaults on those suspected of supporting anarchism. Journalists who professed support for Czolgosz were arrested, and a mob of 100 men from New York City descended upon Paterson, New Jersey, in order to round up and kill the local anarchists that populated that city. As for the assassin himself, Czolgosz was put on trial and summarily convicted. Only six weeks after the shooting of McKinley, Leon Czolgosz was electrocuted, and his corpse covered in quicklime and sulphuric acid in an attempt to destroy it and keep it from relic hunters. Unfortunately this particular mix merely creates plaster of Paris and most likely preserved the killer's body until today.

Perhaps the greatest consequence of McKinley's death was the rise to power of Theodore Roosevelt. The former Rough Rider had been chosen as the party's vice presidential candidate in 1900 largely to remove him from the governorship of New York. During his brief one year in office, he had managed to alienate various conservative and business interests within the Empire State. Thus a move was made by friend and foe alike to have him "promoted" to a position in the federal government. His enemies preferred the position of vice president, as it was a powerless role in which he could be controlled and contained. Clearly no one anticipated the events that were to subsequently transpire that would make Teddy Roosevelt the youngest president in American history.

More important was Roosevelt's adherence to the Progressive movement upon his ascent to power. His youth, aggressive personality, and belief in a square deal for every man prompted him to become the most active chief executive since perhaps Andrew Jackson. Thanks to his forceful leadership, America slowly moved down the road of Progressivism, embracing such concepts as the rise of big government and positive liberty. At the same time his ardent nationalism and internationalism pushed the country even deeper into the imperialism that would define the first quarter of the twentieth century.

Warren G. Harding

Twenty-two years after the death of McKinley, another American president was suddenly felled, continuing the tragic pattern of deaths initiated with the assassination of Abraham Lincoln. The peculiar difference this time, however, was the suddenness and unexplained nature of the demise. Warren G. Harding's death three years into his term of office sparked a number of conspiracy theories both at the time and since, and remains unsatisfactorily explained to this day. Nevertheless, his early death did help to reinvigorate the scandal-damaged Republican Party and perhaps even save them in the election of 1924.

The Solemn Referendum Election of 1920 had put a temporary halt to the Progressivism that had swept the nation like a tempest during the previous twenty years. In many ways Harding himself was a miniature of the Roaring Twenties that was to follow. His frequent use of tobacco and alcohol, his weekly all-night poker games at the White House, and his notorious affairs were an example of the society slowly taking hold across the country. Harding contributed to this thanks to his economic policies and foreign isolationism as well as his personal behavior. Yet the president was far from a healthy man.

On the eve of his election, Harding seems to have been suffering from hypertension and diabetes.[191] He was also beginning to put on weight, and at the time weighed perhaps 200 pounds .Though he took up golf as a form of exercise, much like President Taft, he is frequently recorded as having been out of breath after only a few holes, and would occasionally skip half of the course because he was unable to continue. His notorious golf habit became something of a joke to the American people and was a popular target for his detractors. A newspaper article published shortly after his election prefaced his upcoming visit to the Panama Canal: "Senator Warren G. Harding gave up golfing and motoring this morning to make a personal study of the practical working of the Panama Canal."[192]

In fact Harding's laissez-faire attitude towards his life and health was argued to have been reflected in his management of the White House and nation as well. The notorious Ohio Gang put in place by the president led his administration to be perhaps the most corrupt since Grant's. Harding, a notorious philanderer, was accused of keeping half-a-dozen mistresses and having many affairs while in the White House. The most notorious was perhaps with the young Nan Britton who not only wrote a tell-all book about the affair, but claimed to have had a child with the president. Some of his supporters discounted this at the time, claiming that he was actually sterile due to an episode of mumps orchitis when he was younger that resulted in severe swelling of his testicles.[193] This claim was only further buttressed by his childless marriage to Florence Harding. Yet other mistresses, including Susie Hodder, Rosa Hoyle, and Augusta Cole also claim to have been impregnated by him. As Harding himself once admitted to the National Press Club, "It's a good thing I am not a woman, I would always be pregnant. I can't say no."[194]

Yet the image of Harding as a hands-off administrator more given to golfing and fornication than actual governance is far from the truth. While his opponents may have attempted to portray him as a lackadaisical foil of the hardworking and bookish Wilson, Harding was far more involved in the day-to-day minutia of the federal government. William H. Crawford, in an expose for *McClure's Magazine*, detailed Harding's packed daily schedule. Estimating that the president was working an eighty-four-hour week, contradicting the prominent view that he was an uninvolved leader.[195] The additional stress that this labor caused him could have contributed to the impairment of his health.

The president's eventual downfall came not from political scandal but his choice of physician. His parents had both been well-known practitioners of homeopathic medicine in Ohio. Harding's father, George Tryon Harding, had purchased several books on the topic and attended two classes, which at the time was enough to qualify him for a medical license. His mother, Phoebe, was a homeopathic midwife who was once accused of malpractice following the death of a child in her care. During the subsequent investigation she was cleared, thanks to the help of a fellow homeopath, Charles Sawyer, the man who would eventually become the president's chief physician. Thereafter a loyal friend to the family, Sawyer also became the personal physician to Florence Harding beginning in 1913, seeing her through a number of serious illnesses including a near fatal one in 1916. Her trust in the man is perhaps best demonstrated by her reliance on his advice over that of the famed Dr. Charles Mayo in 1922, when she was suffering from a rather severe urinary infection. On this occasion, newspapers across the country carried hour-by-hour details of her condition. By September 14, the White House itself put out a press communication stating "recovery is not yet assured" for Mrs. Harding, who was suffering acutely by this point.[196] The first lady recovered slowly over the next few months, perhaps more in spite of her care than because of it.

The scandals and lifestyle of the president began to wear on him soon after his arrival in the White House. The alleged bacchanalian orgies at Washington's Little Green House on K Street, including stories of liquor, accidental deaths, blackmail, abortions, gambling, and prostitution, soon began to creep into the public sphere and compromised not only Harding's health but his reputation as well. During his days as a senator Harding was known to be able to sleep or nap in almost any location, but by 1922 he was reported as having to elevate his head with several pillows in order to sleep.[197] Better known as orthopnea, this is normally a telltale sign of congestive heart failure.[198] In January 1923, the president began to experience a severe digestive illness, described at the time as "an attack of the grip," a popular name historically for the flu.[199] The illness, which continued for almost two weeks, was more likely an episode of abdominal angina than influenza, given his subsequent death.

Amidst all of this, the president decided to undertake an epic tour of the western United States to both reinvigorate his image and perhaps his health as well. The Voyage of Understanding, as it was dubbed, would take Harding and his wife from St. Louis to the Territory of Alaska and then down the Pacific Coast to California. The excursion proved to be quite popular, with the president making numerous speeches along the way. After almost three weeks in Alaska, Harding arrived in Vancouver, British Columbia on July 26, 1923. At this point the trip seemed to be taking a toll on his health. He complained of shortness of breath and abdominal pain and was diagnosed by Sawyer with ptomaine poisoning from "a mess of King Crabs drenched in butter." His doctor accordingly began a regime of purgatives to cleanse his digestive system, a move that would have only further strained his already ailing heart. By the end of the month, he was prescribed digitalis and caffeine in an effort to regulate his deteriorating heart rate and blood pressure.

The president continued his journey, delivering a speech in Seattle to 25,000 people. Soon afterwards, the Portland speech was cancelled and

Harding and his retinue quickly moved on to San Francisco where he could rest. It was here in the aptly named Presidential Suite at the Palace Hotel that the president died on August 2, 1923. His wife was reading to him from a newspaper when he suddenly shuddered and expired. Sawyer opined that the cause of death had been a sudden stroke, and the other attending physicians agreed to sign off on this conclusion. Yet it is much more likely that Harding's misdiagnosed heart problems, when combined with Sawyer's general malpractice and recent prescription of purging, led to a massive heart attack and death for the president.

The first lady refused an autopsy, perhaps in a move to protect Sawyer or to hide something else. Upon her own death from renal failure only two years later, rumors quickly began to circulate of a possible plot against the First Family or even the poisoning of Harding by his own wife, either in retaliation for his many years of philandering or in a move to preserve his good name. Gaston B. Means put this theory forward in 1930 in his book *The Strange Death of President Harding*. Still others have argued that the president actually committed suicide, building their case upon his adoption of a new will before leaving Washington for his journey west and his recent sale of his beloved *Marion Star* newspaper. In reality it was the Harding's overreliance on both homeopathic medicine in general and Dr. Sawyer in particular that ultimately doomed the man.

Regardless of the cause of his death, the fallout from it proved to be more interesting. With the removal of Warren G. Harding and most of the notorious Ohio Gang, the White House settled down considerably under the much more taciturn and even-keeled Calvin Coolidge. While the Republican Party had suffered heavy losses during the midterm election of 1922, the new president was able to staunch the bleeding in 1924 and overwhelmingly win the White House. Coolidge's second term in office would continue the small government, laissez-faire ideology of his predecessor, minus the various scandals. The conservative party of the nation was reinvigorated and the Roaring Twenties reached their ultimate height. The death of Harding through the incompetence of his doctor quite possibly saved the party and the decade.

Chapter 7

A MEDICAL AMENDMENT

"Honey, I forgot to duck."
(Ronald Reagan, 1981)

Americans began to awaken to the impact of the health of the president upon the nation more fully with the advent of the Cold War. The idea that nuclear annihilation, or the prevention of it, could depend on the reaction time and health of one individual produced a growing interest on the part of the American public in the physical condition of their commander-in-chief. At the same time, a slew of tell-all books and recent experiences with the health of Franklin D. Roosevelt made both the average citizen and congressmen more wary about believing the rosy pictures of healthy presidents disseminated by the White House. The fact that the era saw two of the oldest men in American history elected to the presidency and numerous elderly candidates who were not, added a touch of urgency to the concern.

Dwight D. Eisenhower

General Dwight D. Eisenhower was the fourth-oldest man to enter the White House at the time of his inauguration in 1953. Since two out of the three men who were older than he—William Henry Harrison and Zachary Taylor—died while in office, his age did cause concern for some citizens. Yet, upon inspection, Ike seemed to be the paradigm of good health. His weight had changed little since West Point, he rarely drank, had quit smoking in 1949, and stayed active by playing golf.[200] What wasn't known to most at the time was that much of this good health was simply an illusion. Eisenhower's four-pack-a-day smoking habit had severely compromised his heart, and led to the heart disease that would trouble him during his time in office. Likewise, ever since his appendectomy in 1923, the general seems to have suffered almost thirty-three years of occasional lower abdominal pain. This condition would not be diagnosed until May 1956, at which point it was realized that he was suffering from Crohn's Disease. Eisenhower, though healthier than Franklin D. Roosevelt, was far from the robust soldier that he was portrayed to be.

The future president's first major brush with illness seems to have occurred in March 1949. Only two months after being inaugurated for a second time, President Harry Truman invited Eisenhower to his summer White House in the Florida Keys. This was part of the president's attempt to woo Ike into serving as an informal chairman of the Joint Chiefs of Staff, a move necessitated more by Eisenhower's prestige than by Truman's devotion to the man. On March 21, the general suffered a sudden illness that was claimed by his doctors to either be a minor heart attack or else a digestive issue. Colonel Dr. Thomas Mattingly, who favored the former diagnosis, later recounted the attempt to deny the episode as being in keeping with the fact that Ike ". . . like many others with aspirations of becoming high-ranking officers and leaders, made special effort to keep his records free of any disease or physical abnormalities which might interfere with subsequent promotions and assignments."[201]

The first whispers about Eisenhower's health occurred well-before the election of 1952. As early as December 1949, while the majority of newspapers and Americans were busy discussing whether Truman would seek a third term, Senator Hubert H. Humphrey opined instead on the potential candidacy of General Eisenhower. Humphrey suggested that Ike could potentially run, but "it probably will depend on his health."[202] Regardless of his concerns, the majority of attention paid to the health of the candidates focused once again upon President Truman. His wife's declining health in 1952 was cited as one of the key reasons that he did not end up seeking a third term in office: "Mr. Truman recently confided to an intimate that Mrs. Truman's high blood pressure just could not stand the excitement of another campaign."[203] Ironically, Bess Truman outlived her husband and every previous first lady as well, dying at the age of ninety-seven in 1982.

Eisenhower himself faced a tough primary challenger in the guise of Senator Robert A. Taft. More aptly known as "Mr. Conservative," Taft had headed the opposition to Franklin Roosevelt's New Deal Coalition and the emerging internationalism of the Democratic and Republican parties beginning with World War II. With the party's disastrous track record running liberal Republicans as candidates between 1936 and 1948, many saw a move to the right by the party to be a better option. The Republican primaries and convention became a running series of bitter fights between the supporters of Ike and Taft. In the end Ike's nomination proved to be the wisest choice for the party, not only because of his wider appeal, but also because of Taft's subsequent death only a few months later. Robert Taft had began to experience lower abdominal pains shortly after Eisenhower's inauguration in January 1953. He was subsequently diagnosed with an unknown cancer, and following an operation in June, died in late July of a brain hemorrhage. An autopsy determined that the senator had succumbed to pancreatic cancer.[204] Had he actually run for president and been elected, Taft would have been unable to accomplish much in office, leaving a vice president which history can only speculate about as the new leader of the nation.

Once elected, the stresses of the Cold War combined with Ike's declining health led to several serious episodes for the president. One of the most severe was on September 24, 1955, while Eisenhower was visiting with his in-laws in Denver. The general had just finished twenty-seven holes of golf and had gone to bed with what he thought was indigestion. Shortly after midnight he awoke, complaining to his wife of chest pains. Dr. Henry Snyder was called to the residence, arriving more than an hour later with oxygen and various medicines, and fought to stabilize his patient. Ike was given amyl nitrate, papaverine, and morphine, and eventually went back to sleep. After awakening again around 11 a.m. experiencing more chest pains, Snyder brought in an electrocardiograph. Upon discovering that the president had most likely experienced a heart attack, he decided to transport him to the local hospital. After almost twenty-four hours of suffering, the president walked to his own limousine and was then driven to Fitzsimmons Army Hospital, where an analysis revealed that Eisenhower had suffered a left anterior myocardial infarction and bore a scar on his heart the size of an olive.[205] The reasons behind Snyder failing to send the president to the hospital earlier remain both a historical mystery and a medical tragedy. While reports varied as to the exact seriousness of his condition, it seems overall to have been a moderate heart attack. The president was kept in an oxygen tent, and wore bright red pajamas with five gold stars on the collar, a gift from the various newsmen who covered him.[206]

Vice President Richard Nixon, the president's wife, and Sherman Adams, who was chief of staff at the time, were all informed immediately of the heart attack, with the rest of the government being filled-in twelve hours later. This relative openness stood in marked contrast to what had transpired during both the Wilson and Roosevelt administrations. The president was to take this transparency with regards to his health even further when he notified his press secretary only two days after his initial heart attack to tell the public everything. There seems to have been no adverse reaction from American citizens to the news, as polls taken in October of that year as to whether Ike should run again recorded that well over 55 percent approved.[207] As part of the campaign to win over the nation, Nixon insisted on employing civilian doctors as well as army medical staff. He stated, "We cannot overlook the fact that many people in the country might have more confidence, however unfounded, in a civilian specialist of national reputation."[208] For this reason, the military brought in renowned cardiologist Dr. Paul Dudley White of Massachusetts General Hospital.

Though the public seems to have taken the heart attack in stride, Wall Street was not as kind. On Monday, September 26, only two days after the incident, the New York Stock Exchange opened and then abruptly collapsed, with the Dow Jones losing 6.5 percent of its value, an estimated $14 billion, its worst loss since 1929. The president's heart attack had put an end to the economic miracle that had begun roughly in 1942 and continued largely unabated until this time. In another sign of fear over the president's condition, Eisenhower's chief physician, Dr. Snyder, began forwarding daily reports to Dr. Eli Ginzberg at Columbia University Hospital in an effort to document his actions and clear his name should the president's health take a turn for the worse. This move was in keeping with Dr. Frank Lahey's precedent of a letter regarding Roosevelt's ability to run back in 1944.

Despite Ike's openness, the White House still carefully managed access to and images of the president. His departure from the hospital in Denver was postponed for several additional weeks until he was able to leave without the aid of a wheelchair. It wouldn't be until November 11 that Eisenhower walked across the tarmac to his waiting plane to fly back to Washington. As late as December, Dr. Snyder was recommending that the president not deliver his State of the Union address in person as it would wear on his health too much. In the intervening weeks, Chief of Staff Adams served as the intermediary between the bedridden president bed and Nixon, who was heading up the cabinet in Washington. Adams' success in these tasks even prompted former President Herbert Hoover, now an elder of the party, to opine during a televised appearance that the Constitution be amended to allow for the creation of a permanent administrative vice president. Regardless of the strength of the idea, its proposal came at a time when such a suggestion was seen as tacit admission of Eisenhower's inability to fulfill his duties as president.[209]

The more interesting historical consequence of these events was the effect of the president's heart attack on the contemporaneous Geneva Summit. Following a series of escalating conflicts in Quemoy and Matsui, the decision of West Germany to join NATO, and the creation of the Warsaw Pact by the USSR, Eisenhower had agreed to an offer by the United Kingdom and France for a four-powers summit at Geneva. The meeting opened in July and discussed such delicate issues as the neutralization of Austria and Ike's Open Skies program. Secretary of State John Foster Dulles rose to the occasion, filling in for the president by assuming a more involved role in the negotiations. Thanks in part to his efforts, a number of notable achievements and agreements were reached.

All of this stands in sharp contrast to the Bermuda Conference held several years earlier in 1953. During his first year in office, Eisenhower was approached by British Prime Minister Winston Churchill, who proposed hosting a three-power summit to discuss the growing West-East conflict. The death of Joseph Stalin and the ascension of Georgy Malenkov led the prime minister to want the meeting to ascertain whether the Russians had developed a "new look," in their foreign policy.[210] Ike was much opposed to the meeting at the time, seeing it merely as a photo-op or window dressing. The still-unresolved issue of Korea was seen to be more of a pressing concern for the administration, while Congress both resented their recent and growing exclusion from foreign affairs and feared the influence of Leftists in the State Department as had occurred at Yalta.[211] Eisenhower considered either cancelling the meeting outright or else inviting Syngman Rhee, president of South Korea, to plead his case for peace in that nation. Luckily for him, Winston Churchill suffered a massive heart attack in January of that year, which left him partially paralyzed on the left side of his body. Though his condition was presented at the time as merely a minor illness, it effectively ended hopes for a conference. Instead the leaders of the United States, the United Kingdom, and France would hold a confab at Bermuda in November in the fall to discuss coordinating their policies towards the Russians. Little would emerge from this dialogue, leaving only speculation as to what a healthier Churchill could have accomplished.

The more pressing issue for Eisenhower became whether to run again in 1956. Numerous commentators described him as depressed in the late fall of 1955, a common side effect in survivors of heart attacks. A controlled diet, a daily regimen of exercise, and the use of the experimental drug Coumadin seemed to convince Ike that the burdens of office might be too much. His own vice president, Richard Nixon, would write years later, "He went through a long period of deep depression. He talked like a man who felt his public career was finished. He did not even want to discuss the possibility of running the following year."[212] The Republican establishment was understandably worried about their chances should the very popular president not run again: "The Republican national chairman, Len Hall, was naturally terrified. When reporters asked him about the election, his stock reply was that the ticket would be Ike and Dick. Finally, one reporter asked the dreaded question: 'What happens if Eisenhower decides not to run?' Hall blurted out, 'We will jump off that bridge when we come to it.'"[213] On December 26, 1955, Eisenhower himself opined that Nixon should perhaps run instead of him. In fact, as far back as his inaugural address in 1953, the new president had pushed to include a one-term promise in his address.[214] Some commentators went so far as to suggest that not only should Ike not run again, but that he should step down from office immediately for the good of the nation. One newspaper wrote, "Dwight Eisenhower has been trained as a soldier. His sense of duty will determine his future."[215]

Events evolved rapidly in 1956. Ike was still not convinced that Nixon was ready for the burdens of the office due in part to his young age at the time.[216] The president called together a secret meeting on January 3, 1956, during which he consulted his advisors as to the proper course of action to follow. The general consensus was that they had full faith in Ike's ability to weather a second term. Polls taken in key states at the same time showed a similar opinion among the general population.[217] The president slowly made up his mind over the next few weeks to seek a second term. On February 14, after performing a follow-up examination, Dr. Paul Dudley White, Ike's Harvard-educated cardiologist, told the press that Eisenhower could continue "his present active life satisfactorily for another five to ten years." Yet at the same time, White privately urged the president not to run. The very fact that Ike had to announce his intentions stood in sharp contrast to almost every other sitting president over the previous seventy years, whose re-nomination was seen as simply a *fait accompli*.

As the election rematch between Eisenhower and Adlai Stevenson raged on, the president was once again taken ill. In the early hours of June 8, 1956, Ike awoke and complained to his wife of lower abdominal pains. Dr. Howard Snyder arrived a half-hour later and noted moderate distention and tympanites, but no other symptoms. He quickly ruled out a heart issue and continued to observe the patient throughout the morning, blaming indigestion for Eisenhower's illness. A series of tap water enemas were employed once the sun had come up, but the pain seemed only to grow more intense and localized. At 10:30 a.m. Ike vomited up about 1.5 liters of bile and his blood pressure began to drop.

A sugar solution drip was soon administered and the decision was made to move the president by ambulance to Walter Reed Hospital. Various heart specialists were called in, including White, to assess Eisenhower's condition. It was soon determined that he had been felled by a case of Crohn's ileitis, a constriction of the intestine that had actually been observed a month before by his physicians. At that time, the doctors decided to keep the diagnosis from the president, as it was feared it would have caused him undue strain.[218] No one on the medical team was willing to suggest surgery as a solution, and Mamie Eisenhower was adamantly opposed to it. Finally, with X-rays showing the distention of the president's lower bowel to be getting progressively worse, Snyder browbeat the attending physicians into agreeing to operate, and the president's son signed the necessary paperwork. The surgery went smoothly. An ileotransverse colostomy bypassed the blocked or damaged section of his ileum. While some in the medical community balked at the idea that the diseased portion of his intestine was not removed, his doctors argued that additional surgeries would have endangered the president's already frail health and kept him from returning to the White House for months.[219] As it was, in less than a week he was back to work and in three weeks was discharged from the hospital.

The election of 1956 continued unabated as the president slowly recovered. The Republicans initially sought to rely heavily upon television as a medium by which the sickened president could address the nation. Numerous commercials and speeches were utilized to limit the strain on Eisenhower. Predictably enough, this simply increased concerns among the public that the sitting president was too infirm to campaign, let alone govern the nation. Democrats seized upon this fear, running a short commercial which asked Americans whether they were "Nervous about Nixon? President Nixon?" Adlai Stevenson himself announced that he would not publically make the health of the president an issue during the campaign.[220]

The Republicans responded to these health concerns by pushing Ike out into the field. As he always did, the president responded strongly, giving speeches and meeting people. As younger brother Milton Eisenhower succinctly put it, "it doesn't matter what you say." Eisenhower simply had to appear healthy and in command.[221] All of this campaigning had a deleterious effect on Ike's health. Over the course of a little more than a month, he developed a persistent cough, heart palpitations, abdominal pain, dizziness, and diarrhea. None of this though could prevent his unparalleled popularity from securing forty-one states and 57 percent of the popular vote, two more states than in 1952.

Though the president breezed into a second term, his health continued to play havoc on his time in office. While an official physical undertaken in early November 1957 portrayed him in good health and recovering from both his cardiac and intestinal issues, he was in actuality on the verge of a greater attack. Only a few weeks later, in late November, during a visit to the White House by the king of Morocco, Eisenhower had just settled down to work when he found himself unable to read or grasp a pen. He also discovered that he could not talk, once he had hastily summoned his personal secretary. Dr. Snyder and others discovered that Ike had experienced a stroke due to an occlusion of the left middle cerebral artery. The press was once again made fully aware of the situation, though the incident was described as only "a little stroke."[222] By the next day, *The New York Times* was already reporting that Eisenhower was shaving himself and had signed twelve official documents.

As always, the truth about the president's recovery was far from rosy. Though he was to suffer no major motor or sensory damage, his speech was markedly different after this incident. Personal fears led Ike to draft a secret letter to Nixon in February 1958, authorizing him, in the event of a serious health issue, to become acting president as long as Eisenhower remained incapacitated. The letter mentioned the health issues of both James Garfield and Woodrow Wilson, but seemed destined to lead to a constitutional crisis, as it allowed Nixon himself to decide if the president were infirm. Ever true to the idea of transparency that permeated his entire administration, and perhaps due to a mistrust of Nixon, Eisenhower released the letter to the public by the end of the month, reassuring the nation and its enemies of an orderly transition should the unthinkable happen.

Eisenhower somehow survived the last two years in office and then slowly settled into retirement. He lived for another eight years, and died of heart failure in March 1969. His popularity suffered significantly in the first few decades after his departure from office. For years he was largely seen as a caretaker president who presided over lackluster attempts to confront the growing civil and foreign policy problems of the nation. Undoubtedly some of this arose from his health issues while in office.

The Twenty-fifth Amendment

The collective apprehension of the nation and its political class over the issue of continuity in government reached a height in the 1960s. The illnesses and incapacities of James Garfield, Woodrow Wilson, Franklin Roosevelt, and Dwight Eisenhower increased calls for an amendment to address this concern. The final impetus seems to have been the assassination of John F. Kennedy and Lyndon Johnson's own heart issues upon assuming power in 1963, both during an increasingly volatile period of the Cold War.[223]

Prior to 1967, numerous pieces of legislation had laid out the proper succession should the president, vice president, or other members of the government perish while in office.[224] These mostly concerned themselves with the proper order of succession, resolving the "who" but not the "when" and "how" of the issue. Though Article II, Section 1, Clause 6 of the Constitution provides: "The Congress may by Law provide for the Case of Removal, Death, Resignation or Inability, both of the President and Vice President, declaring what Officer shall then act as President, and such Officer shall act accordingly, until the Disability be removed, or a President shall be elected," the meaning of how Congress would do that remained unclear. For example, in the case of Woodrow Wilson, the Congress was unaware as to the extent of the president's condition, and his closest advisors and physician refused to devolve power onto anyone else.

Some presidents had designed their own methods for the transference of power. As has already been discussed, the informal agreement between Eisenhower and Nixon was an understandable attempt to resolve the issue, but one fraught with constitutional concerns. A similar situation unfolded in October 1965, when President Lyndon Johnson underwent gall bladder and throat surgery and had to turn power over to Vice President Hubert Humphrey. Johnson consulted with Eisenhower in this process, hoping to ascertain the best way to inform the American public about the procedure. The president had lost more than twenty pounds since September, and though his condition was portrayed to be a less serious one, there was still notable concern among the general public. Johnson made sure to issue his announcement to the nation after the stock market had closed for the day, no doubt having learned from the mistake of Ike a decade before. In the end, the two-hour operation went without incident and Humphrey's time as acting president was uneventful.

A number of proposals began to arise in the 1960s to address this weakness. Prominent among these were the Keating-Kefauver and Bayh-Celler proposals, the first of which granted the power to Congress to determine the ability of the president to remain in office, and the latter of which moved that responsibility over to the Executive branch. Bayh-Celler eventually passed both houses of Congress and went next to the states, where between 1965 and 1967 it was ratified and subsequently enacted as the Twenty-fifth Amendment to the Constitution.

The amendment addressed a number of historical and immediate concerns. President John Tyler's assumption of power as "president" rather than simply "acting president" was declared to be the new constitutional norm. Secondly, the amendment made possible the filling of vacancies in the office of vice president, a pressing concern in Cold War. More important, though, were the contents of Sections 3 and 4, which spelled out the process for declaring the president incapable of continuing in office. Section 3 provides: Whenever the President transmits to the President pro tempore of the Senate and the Speaker of the House of Representatives his written declaration that he is unable to discharge the powers and duties of his office, and until he transmits to them a written declaration to the contrary, such powers and duties shall be discharged by the Vice President as Acting President.

This is similar to the process undertaken by Eisenhower in early 1958 following his stroke. More controversial, however, is Section 4, which also provides for the removal of the president by both the vice president and the cabinet:

Whenever the Vice President and a majority of either the principal officers of the executive departments or of such other body as Congress may by law provide, transmit to the President pro tempore of the Senate and the Speaker of the House of Representatives their written declaration that the President is unable to discharge the powers and duties of his office, the Vice President shall immediately assume the powers and duties of the office as Acting President.

Thereafter, when the President transmits to the President pro tempore of the Senate and the Speaker of the House of Representatives his written declaration that no inability exists, he shall resume the powers and duties of his office unless the Vice President and a majority of either the principal officers of the executive department or of such other body as Congress may by law provide, transmit within four days to the President pro tempore of the Senate and the Speaker of the House of Representatives their written declaration that the President is unable to discharge the powers and duties of his office. Thereupon Congress shall decide the issue, assembling within forty-eight hours for that purpose if not in session. If the Congress, within twenty-one days after receipt of the latter written declaration, or, if Congress is not in session, within twenty-one days after Congress is required to assemble, determines by two-thirds vote of both Houses that the President is unable to discharge the powers and duties of his office, the Vice President shall continue to discharge the same as Acting President; otherwise, the President shall resume the powers and duties of his office.

Though this article was aimed at providing a means by which to prevent another Wilson-type situation, the mechanism was not without its constitutional and practical issues. While the Legislative branch is removed from the initial decision as to the transfer of power to the vice president, a scenario where a power struggle erupted between the president and vice president is imaginable.

Since its ratification, the Twenty-fifth Amendment has been utilized on several occasions. In fact only six years after its adoption, it helped to carry out Nixon's resignation from office. His first vice president, Spiro T. Agnew, had been forced to step down in October 1973 because of accusations of tax evasion. Rather than leave a vacancy in the Executive branch, Section 2 of the amendment was invoked, and Congress confirmed House Minority Leader Gerald Ford as vice president. Little more than a year later, in accordance with Section 1 of the amendment, Ford assumed the presidency when Nixon resigned. Shortly afterwards, Congress confirmed Nelson Rockefeller vice president. If the amendment had never been adopted, then under the Succession Act of 1947 Speaker of the House Carl Albert, a Democrat from Oklahoma, would have become president following Nixon's departure. Albert could also have blocked the vote to approve Ford as vice president, thereby creating a constitutional crisis and paving the way for his own rise to the presidency. This clearly highlighted another issue with the amendment. A move to repeal the amendment in 1974, in a bill introduced by Rep. Julia Butler Hansen (D-Washington), started to build support due to the very undemocratic way by which Ford rose to presidency. Speaker Albert, when questioned as to the wisdom of the repeal, stated "that will be very popular."[225]

Section 3 of the amendment has been invoked on three occasions since its ratification, all for predictable and minor medical procedures. One was on June 29, 2002, and another on July 21, 2007, both within the presidency of George W. Bush. The president underwent two separate colonoscopies and both times submitted letters to Congress transferring power temporarily to the vice president. On both occasions Dick Cheney was vested with presidential powers for a little more than two hours. While neither declaration was probably necessary, coming as it did during the War on Terror, Bush felt that continuity in command must be preserved. Regardless, both transitions were flawless and demonstrated the effectiveness of that section of the amendment.

Ronald Reagan

The most serious test for the Twenty-fifth Amendment arose in the 1980s during the presidency of Ronald Reagan. When inaugurated in 1981, he was the oldest man yet to enter the White House. At only sixteen days short of his seventieth birthday, he was almost two years older than William Henry Harrison and six years older than Zachary Taylor, both of whom died while in office. Yet despite some concerns from the public, he was acknowledged to be in good health. To help calm the fears of voters, Reagan himself pledged in June 1980 to have periodic checkups while in office, vowing to resign immediately should a doctor find him no longer fit to carry on the burdens of the position.[226]

With the major economic, social, and foreign policy issues of the day polling ahead of the age and health of the candidates as a concern, Reagan swept into office. He was in power for little more than two months when he was severely injured in an assassination attempt. After having just visited Ford's Theater a little more than a week before, Reagan was the target of an attack by John Hinckley Jr. while standing outside the Hilton Hotel in Washington D.C. At 2:30 p.m. on March 30, 1981, after delivering an address before the AFL-CIO, the president was hit by a bullet in his chest under his left arm. The shot itself actually ricocheted off of the bullet-proof window of his presidential limo. It was the fifth bullet that

Hinckley fired, and by that time the Secret Service had already thrown Reagan into the limo and sped off. A few seconds later, the president felt pain in his chest but assumed it was only a bruised or broken rib caused by his rough entrance into the car. When the president began to cough up blood and found himself struggling to breathe, the Secret Service ordered him to be driven to George Washington University Hospital rather than to the White House. That decision most likely saved his life.

Though Reagan was allowed to walk into the hospital on his own, he barely made it into the building before he collapsed. A quick examination by Dr. Wesley Price found the entrance wound below Reagan's left armpit but no exit wound. Tests of his vitals showed an extremely weak pulse and signs of strained breathing due to his collapsed lung. The president was given oxygen, two units of blood, and his wife was brought in as he was prepared for emergency surgery. It was at this point that Reagan turned to the first lady and whispered, "Honey, I forgot to duck."

Dr. Joseph Giordano inserted tubes into the president's chest to drain out any fluid that was present. To his horror, blood started to pour from the tubes, with Reagan eventually losing around 80 fluid ounces, about half of what was in his body. By 3:24 p.m. the president was wheeled into the operating room while receiving blood almost continuously to staunch his bleeding. Reagan turned to the doctors and weakly mumbled, "Please tell me you're all Republicans," after which point he was anesthetized.

The operation to save his life would last until around 6:20 that evening. The doctors were able to stop his bleeding, repair the damage to his lung, and after a difficult search find and remove the dime-sized, flattened bullet which had buried itself in some tissue about an inch from the heart. By the time his wounds were closed, the president had lost some 115 ounces of blood. All told, his wound was worse than those received by James Garfield or William McKinley, but thanks to his proximity to a modern hospital and the skill of his doctors, Reagan survived.

Shockingly, no move was made to initiate the protocols of the Twenty-fifth Amendment. In fact at 7:15 a.m. the next morning, President Reagan even signed a piece of farming legislation. Despite this blatant attempt at showing that he was still in complete control of the situation, the president continued to pass in and out of consciousness for days, while at the same time coughing up blood and still struggling to breathe. On April 2, his temperature suddenly spiked. X-rays showed either bleeding or an infection in his lower left lung. Aggressive treatments continued until April 5, at which point his condition improved enough for him to receive briefings. Only three days later he was discharged from the hospital and was able to walk into the White House under his own power. Ten days after the assassination attempt, President Reagan was home, but he was inattentive, weak, and unable to concentrate for weeks. Not surprisingly, it was difficult for a man of his age to recover quickly from such a physically damaging and mentally traumatizing event. As a visitor to the White House observed, the president was "pale and disoriented . . . walking with the hesitant steps of an old man."[227]

During the almost month-long period of Reagan's initial recovery, it is not clear who was actually running the Executive branch. Vice President George H. W. Bush headed cabinet meetings, but for the most part the government seemed to simply be on autopilot. The day of the assassination, as Vice President Bush was flying over Texas and reporters at the White House were demanding answers, Secretary of State Alexander Haig told the press, "Constitutionally, gentlemen, you have the president, the vice president and the secretary of state, in that order, and should the president decide he wants to transfer the helm to the vice president, he will do so. He has not done that. As of now, I am in control here, in the White House." Not only was this not true with regards to the Constitution; it presented to both the nation and our enemies a dangerous split within the government.

Haig had been jockeying for more power since Reagan's inauguration and had battled heatedly with both George Bush and Richard V. Allen, the national security advisor. The timing of the attack on the president proved to be dangerous as massive strikes were breaking out in Poland, and Soviet subs were patrolling closer to the East Coast. A fight broke out in the Situation Room between Haig and Secretary of Defense Caspar Weinberger over the degree of response by American nuclear forces in response to Russia's aggressive moves. Only the arrival of the vice president hours later returned continuity to the Executive branch. Without the activation of the Twenty-fifth Amendment and without the presence of the Speaker of the House or president *pro tem-*

pore of the Senate, Haig was perhaps right. Yet his failure to contact these two men raises many questions.[228]

More alarming was the fact that when the FBI seized Reagan's clothes and possessions as evidence, they unknowingly took the nuclear launch card the president always carried in his wallet to authenticate a nuclear strike against the USSR should war suddenly break out. Had Moscow responded to Reagan's condition by launching a decapitation strike, would Bush have been able to reply?

Perhaps learning from this episode, Reagan took extra precautions during a series of surgeries in 1985. Having discovered the presence of polyps and a tumor during a colonoscopy, the president opted for surgery on July 13, 1985. While not specifically invoking Section 3 of the Twenty-fifth Amendment, Reagan notified both the Speaker of the House and president *pro tempore* of the Senate that he was temporarily handing over executive authority to Vice President Bush. In his notification letter, Reagan himself noted, "I do not believe that the drafters of this Amendment intended its application to situations such as the instant one . . . and not intending to set a precedent binding anyone privileged to hold this Office in the future," he would conduct the handover of his own accord.[229] After a three-hour operation to remove the tumor, Reagan was once again in control of the Executive branch.

Ronald Reagan underwent numerous other minor procedures during his time in office, none of which drastically affected his presidency. Three of these occurred in 1987 alone and involved a further colonoscopy, an operation to remove a small area of skin cancer, and a transurethral prostate surgery.

Yet the most controversial health issue of Reagan's time in office remains his bout with Alzheimer's Disease. While it is clear that the president was stricken with the ailment during the 1990s, and that complications from it would ultimately lead to his death, the exact starting point of the condition remains nebulous and debated. Reagan did not officially disclose the illness until November 1994, when he wrote an open letter to the American public informing them, "I have recently been told that I am one of the millions of Americans who will be afflicted with Alzheimer's Disease."[230] Despite his use of the future tense in this declaration, the prediction of Alzheimer's was impossible at this time.

Some, including one of the president's sons, have attempted to push the onset of the disease back into his time in the White House. Several contemporary observers and many more recent Epimethei have attempted to identify every moment of confusion during his eight years in office as positive proof of early onset Alzheimer's. One of the more popular moments was during the first debate of the 1984 presidential election where Reagan was seen as worn down and confused. Yet during the second debate, the president himself issued the famous promise, not to make age an issue by calling into question Mondale's youth or inexperience. One should keep in mind that Reagan was by profession a trained actor, which would undoubtedly have helped to cover up any early signs.

By 1987 it appears that there was a movement among several key players within the White House to sideline Reagan. The main person behind this was Howard Baker, the president's newest chief of staff. As detailed in *Landslide: The Unmaking of the President*, an initial fact-finding investigation by Baker and his aide James Cannon revealed a president who was inept, out of touch, and forgetful. Talk even turned to invoking the Twenty-fifth Amendment to remove the president from power. However, on the fateful day of Reagan's arrival at an inquisition chaired by Baker, the president so impressed all of those present that any thoughts of forcing his early retirement were abandoned. Once again, was the president suffering from Alzheimer's, or were the charges against him more in line with his hands-off approach to government?

Chapter 8

A CAMELOT OF CONTAGION

"Nobody's able to figure what's wrong with me. All they do
is talk about what an interesting case."
(John F. Kennedy, 1934)

To many Americans, John F. Kennedy represented the promise and vitality of their generation. The handover of power from the sickly and elderly Eisenhower to the youthful Kennedy was symbolic of the rise of the Greatest Generation to power, a position they would hold until 1992. The White House was to be occupied by a junior naval officer from World War II rather than a general, a man with a young and growing family as opposed to one with grandchildren, and a man in the prime of his life and health rather than a perennial sufferer of heart disease. A cursory glance at one of the new president's campaign commercials serves to illustrate this point. Amidst a catchy, repetitive refrain and various cartoon images, JFK is described as a man who is "young enough to do." Once in office, the media and public's obsession with Camelot, the name sometimes used when referring to Kennedy's presidency, only further pushed this narrative, focusing on the active lifestyle of the first family. But the true nature of Kennedy's health was far from such a rosy and idealized picture. In reality the president suffered from numerous ailments throughout his life that brought him into politics, severely impacted his time in office, and helped to cause his death.

It has been recently speculated that the various illnesses that afflicted Kennedy were not isolated in nature, but were in reality a direct result of his suffering from autoimmune polyendocrine syndrome type II, or APS II.[231] This disorder, which is most likely of genetic origin, can be connected to many of the health issues that arose during his lifetime, including

Addison's, hypothyroidism, pernicious anemia, myasthenia gravis, colitis, and many others. Additionally, according to Dr. Janet Travell, who served as Kennedy's personal physician, he was born with the left side of his body smaller than the right. This condition, reminiscent of the equally tragic Richard III, would contribute to the numerous, painful back issues that plagued him during his life. Arguably, as will be discussed later, his APS II and back issues were also in part responsible for his untimely death.

Among the Kennedy family, Jack was known as a rather sickly child. By the age of two, he had already been stricken with scarlet fever that almost killed him, measles, whooping cough, and chicken pox. Before he left childhood, he also experienced episodes of jaundice, German measles, and had his tonsils removed. In 1931, while attending the Canterbury School in Connecticut, Kennedy required an appendectomy and soon after left the institution. For high school, the future president matriculated at the Choate School. Here his health only further declined thanks to an episode of painful colitis. Treatments of his illness appear to have been severe, with him once writing to his roommate Lem Billings, "I've got something wrong with my intestines. In other words I shit blood. Yesterday I went through the most harassing experience of my life. [A doctor] stuck an iron tube 12 inches long and 1 inch in diameter up my ass. . . . My poor bedraggled rectum is looking at me very reproachfully these days. . . . The reason I'm here is that they may have to cut out my stomach!"[232] Kennedy's colitis would go on to trouble him throughout his life and help to shape its course.

After finishing at Choate, young Jack Kennedy traveled to England where he enrolled at the London School of Economics. Yet little more than a month into his time at the prestigious institution, an attack of jaundice forced him to cut his educational career short and return home to America. A late arrival at Princeton University was also subsequently cut short due to illness and Kennedy was once more hospitalized. From 1936 to 1941, he was in relatively good health and was able to finally earn a degree from Harvard University followed by extensive travel in Europe and South America. As the second Kennedy son and a sickly youth, Joseph P. Kennedy placed less attention on Jack than he did on the molding of older brother Joseph Jr.

As America drew closer towards involvement in World War II, John F. Kennedy sought to enlist in the army. However his various illnesses and back problems kept him from being accepted into the service. In fact his back problems had grown bad enough by 1938 to require the frequent use of a back brace. Likewise he seems to have contracted at least one STD by this point, chlamydia, and was being treated with sulfa.[233] Hoping to build up a future political career for his son, Joseph P. Kennedy managed to call in several favors and have Jack admitted into the navy in September 1941, a travesty of political string-pulling. During his time in the military, Kennedy was once more treated for colitis. His well-known, though controversial, war record and heroic actions in the Solomon Islands only further exacerbated his back problems, as he helped to swim a wounded comrade to a distant island, which left him with a case of malaria. Though Kennedy attempted to hide his increasingly troublesome back and stomach ailments in order to be assigned to another PT boat, he would not receive the posting.[234] By 1944, JFK was back in the United States, receiving treatment for both his back as well as his colitis. Both ailments would eventually force him out of the military.

In the 1940s, John F. Kennedy began a regimen of drug use that increased as the decades wore on. For some undisclosed reason, he began taking steroids at some point between 1937 and 1944. Some historians, most notably Robert Dallek, have postulated that Jack began to use DOCA pellets that he directly injected into his skin as early as his Harvard days. Evidence from his 1944 back operation seems to support this possibility as his surgeons reportedly noticed significant osteoporosis in his lower back, a condition that could result from frequent and prolonged use of steroids.[235] His decades-long use and overuse of the drug would also produce a condition known as moon faces in which the patient develops a fat, rounded facial appearance. Worse than the effect on Kennedy's infamous vanity, steroid abuse could also have led to additional health issues, including, possibly, his Addison's disease. JFK was also taking iodine, most likely for hypothyroidism, another condition associated with his APS II. It has also been established that he was on a daily testosterone regimen, though whether this was for hypogonadism or as an adjunct to simply just to keep his weight up is unknown. The effects of this drug on his already legendary libido, however, can only be speculated upon.

After the end of World War II and following the death of his eldest son, Joseph P. Kennedy quickly arranged for the political rise of JFK. In 1946, Jack was elected to the House of Representatives from a safely

Democratic district in Massachusetts. His six years in the House were almost completely dominated by his health issues. In 1947, while on a trip to London, he was diagnosed as suffering from Addison's disease, an endocrine disorder most likely brought about by his APS II. The English doctors felt that his condition was so far gone that he was given less than a year to live. In fact shortly afterwards, while returning home aboard the *Queen Mary*, Kennedy fell so terribly ill that he was given last rites upon disembarking in Boston, the first of three times this would occur. Undoubtedly this ever-present specter of death weighed heavily on him, and perhaps contributed to some of his actions and thoughts, especially his legendary philandering. Regardless, it also set in motion the health cover-up that would follow JFK for the next fifteen years.

Though he did not die, his declining health continued as his collapsing spine competed with his Addison's and colitis to destroy him. His time in the House proved to be completely mediocre, due in part to his frequent hospitalization. Despite this, Kennedy was still able to get elected to the Senate in 1952. His two terms in this august body were more occupied with surgeries and health scares than with actual legislative accomplishments. The most serious episode came in 1954, when his deteriorating spinal health necessitated yet another surgery. His recovery was complicated by another urinary tract infection, which sent him into a coma and again led to his receiving last rites. Over the course of the next three years alone, from 1955 to 1957, he would return to the hospital a total of nine times for a variety of reoccurring ailments.[236] Throughout all this the Kennedy team organized an effective cover-up campaign to disguise the extent of his maladies. Nevertheless his time in the hospital led him to miss a number of important votes, including the one to censure Senator Joseph McCarthy. The young Kennedy was the only Democratic member not to cast his vote against McCarthy, for which Eleanor Roosevelt in particular leveled criticism against him.[237] Interestingly, given that Joseph P. Kennedy had once donated $30,000 to McCarthy, this missed vote may have had less to do with illness than politics.

Kennedy's next hurdle with his frail health came during his campaign for the presidency in 1960. During the hard fought primary, supporters of Lyndon B. Johnson and others assailed the health of the senator from Massachusetts. His Addison's in particular was mentioned with former

DNC Vice President India Edwards commenting that Kennedy "looked like a spavined hunchback."[239] Still other Democrats questioned his drug use and the impact it had on both his physical and mental health. Future Texas governor John Connally, then a faithful Johnson ally, took it one step further, lamenting that Kennedy wouldn't actual finish his term as "he was going to die."[240] To counter these damning claims, the Kennedy campaign put out a letter from its medical team stating that JFK did not suffer from Addison's caused by tuberculosis. This was in effect true, as his Addison's was caused by either steroid abuse or his APS II, but it was clearly a sly manipulation of his medical history. He was able to clinch the Democratic nomination in the end and, surprising many, chose Lyndon Baines Johnson as his running mate, a man who had himself only recently survived a heart attack. While historians have generally surmised this choice was out of political necessity to balance the ticket, the reason that Johnson chose to accept has been more elusive. The rampant speculation at the time that, much like with FDR in 1944, JFK's running mate would eventually become president, may have prompted the sudden willingness by Johnson to sign on to the Kennedy ticket despite their acrimonious past.

Kennedy's competition with Richard Nixon during the election that year saw his health brought to the fore. The Democratic candidate was kept in action by a competent support team that included medical help as well. An aide followed Kennedy around with a black bag filled with various medications. For obvious reasons, the existence of this valet was kept secret from almost everyone. While campaigning in Connecticut only forty-eight hours before the election, Kennedy's people lost his medical bag, causing fear and chaos among his staff. The candidate himself called up Governor Abraham Ribicoff to say, "There's a medical bag floating around and it can't get in anybody's hands. . . . You have to find that bag . . . it would be murder."[241] Nixon was no less willing to use Kennedy's illnesses against him than Johnson had been. In episodes eerily foreshadowing the Watergate break-in, the offices of two of JFK's doctors were ransacked in the fall of 1960, including that of future White House physician Janet Travell. Luckily for the Democratic candidate, his records were filed under a pseudonym. Shortly before the election, Representative Walter Judd of Minnesota, who had given the keynote speech at the

Republican National Convention, challenged Kennedy to reveal the true depth of his ailments. Thanks to his subterfuge, JFK was able to portray himself as an energetic healthy campaigner, and for the most part was able to dodge this inquisition. On the other hand, Nixon's own knee injury, refusal to accept make up, and a vicious staphylococcal infection doomed his televised debate with Kennedy and probably contributed to his loss in the election.

Kennedy's brief time in the White House was made possible by his indomitable nature, his frequent spirit-lifting dalliances, and his daily cocktail of medicines. Dr. Travell recorded that by 1961, the president's daily regimen included vitamin C, prednisone, methyltestosterone, cortisone, liothyronine, lomotil, paregoric, phenobarbital, trasentine, procaine, various antibiotics, and Tuinal as well as his usual drugs for Addison's and his steroids. Alarmingly, a number of these pills and injections contained opium or were mood-altering substances. Beginning in 1961, the infamous Dr. Max Jacobson, better known as "Dr. Feelgood" to his numerous Hollywood and political patients, began prescribing amphetamines to the president. Kennedy soon depended heavily on these drugs to keep him going in the White House, and granted Jacobson unparalleled access to both the Executive Mansion as well as to himself. In 1961 and 1962 alone, Dr. Feelgood visited the White House no fewer than thirty times and was flown to see the president in numerous other locations as well.[242] Jacobson even accompanied Kennedy to Vienna in 1961, for his first interaction with Khrushchev, a summit that even JFK later admitted went terribly for him.

The effect of all of these illnesses and drugs on the presidency of John F. Kennedy can only be speculated. Close inspections of the most important moments of his three years in office clearly reveal close interactions, even if not causation between the two. On April 17, 1961, as CIA-trained Cuban exiles stormed the beaches of Cuba, the president was receiving 600,000 units of penicillin to fight an STD flair-up. After the failure of the Bay of Pigs operation, his medical records show treatment for acute diarrhea as well as depression. One historian even suggests that Kennedy was under the influence of amphetamines when he made his famous Berlin speech.[243] Not everyone within the administration welcomed the help of Dr. Jacobson or the prospect of a drug-addled commander-in-chief so close to nuclear exchange with the Soviets. Dr. Hans Kraus appealed to Kennedy in December 1962, "No president with his finger on the red button has any business taking stuff like that."[244] As for Jacobson, by 1969 the New York Bureau of Narcotics and Dangerous Drugs had seized most of his supplies, and he lost his license in 1975 after becoming hooked on amphetamines himself.

In a way, one of Kennedy's earliest illnesses contributed to his short life. On the morning of November 22, 1963, Kennedy put on his usual stiff back brace that helped to relieve the pain that would result from his having to sit upright for too long. The brace tended to immobilize him, but as he was to be riding in a car with Governor John Connally of Texas, he felt that it would not present a problem. At 12:30 p.m. that day, as the president's limo drove through Dealey Plaza, a gunshot rang out and a bullet pierced Kennedy, entering through his back and exiting from his throat. The wound was damaging, but not fatal. However, his back brace kept him from falling forward and thus made him an easy target for the bullet fired shortly thereafter. This shot hit the president's head, causing a fatal wound. Kennedy's assassin had a ready accomplice in the president's back brace.

Interestingly, though much has been made of the Warren Commission covering up the true events surrounding the assassination, the biggest lies seem to have centered on omissions regarding his health. The official autopsy performed at the Naval Medical School in Bethesda, Maryland, was quite in-depth with its analysis of the corpse. Yet despite the apparent professionalism of the doctors, no mention was made of Kennedy's non-existent adrenal glands. In 1967, Dr. John Nichols, who had done much research into the president's health issues, wrote a journal article in which he attacked both the autopsy and the commission for leaving out this information, which pointed to Kennedy's Addison's.[245] The reasons for this blatant omission can only be speculated at, but most likely seem to concern a desire to preserve the untarnished image of the late president's strength, youth, and virility.

Chapter 9

MY KINGDOM FOR A CURE

"I won't pick on an invalid."
(Ronald Reagan, 1988)

The often invisible, or at least unnoticed, nature of illness often re-moved it as a determining factor in elections. Only in cases where the ailment was quite obvious did the American public historically take it into consideration when deciding their candidate or casting their bal-lot. In the absence of any telltale sign of disease, some voters sought to rely upon age instead as a gauge of a candidate's health. Thus the wisdom acquired from years of experience often had to contend with the inevi-tability of death in the minds of the public. As discussed in Chapter Two, the illness of William H. Crawford not only kept him from becoming president, but also helped to once again usher a two-party system into the country. Crawford was not alone as a candidate whose seemingly assured rise to power was brought to a sudden halt by injury or illness. Disease not only shaped those men who made it to the White House, but kept others out as well.

The Election of 1812

Perhaps the first instance of illness playing a role in the shaping of an elec-tion came about in 1812. The Republicans had enjoyed control of the White House for twelve years, ever since Jefferson's Revolution of 1800, a position they seemed destined to maintain into the immediate future. Though Federalist fortunes were waning for a number of reasons, the slow slouch towards war against the United Kingdom bolstered the par-ty's support in the North. This region would be on the front line of any

invasion of Canada, and would suffer immensely should the British re-
taliate or push the American army back. Understanding the questionable
popularity of the recently-launched conflict, James Madison was planning
to use his reelection as a referendum on it. Opposition to his ideas would
not come from the Federalist Party alone.

Many northern Republicans resented the near universal dominance
of the South in general, and Virginia in particular, over the party. At the
same time, others within the party felt that Madison was only lukewarm
on war with Britain and lacked the decisiveness to win the struggle.[246]
Support began to shift from the president to Vice President George Clinton. The latter was an ardent anti-Federalist who had led the state of New
York throughout the Revolutionary War and had been a personal friend
of George Washington. Clinton had served as vice president under both
Jefferson and Madison and even managed to receive six electoral votes
for president in the election of 1808. Not only did Clinton have ample
support in the North, but his age and military experience were clear
advantages over Madison. General Henry Dearborn feared the influence
of Clinton enough to discuss the issue with Thomas Jefferson, writing,
"The Clinton party are hostile & active . . . rendering the measures of the
President unpopular, or his reelection doubtfull."[247]

As the Republican congressmen were beginning to meet and discuss
a candidate for the election, Clinton's health began to fail him. Dolley
Madison described him as "dangerously ill" at the end of March.[248] Several weeks later, on April 20, 1812, Vice President Clinton suffered a massive
heart attack and died in Washington. Anti-Madison Republicans rushed
to find a replacement candidate and soon settled on the now-deceased
vice president's nephew, DeWitt Clinton. The new contender had only
recently been made mayor of New York City and had very little experience or support behind him, besides his surname. Though the Federalists
did not officially support Clinton, they would overwhelmingly vote for
him. The fusion candidate went on to tailor his message to various groups
from which he hoped to gain support, one day lambasting Madison's handling of the war while the next day speaking out against the conflict itself.

Madison just managed to be re-elected, securing barely more than
half of the popular vote. DeWitt Clinton gained the traditional Federalist
states of New England as well as New York, a state they had not taken

since 1796. In fact had Pennsylvania gone fusion, Madison would have been defeated. It is interesting to speculate what course George Clinton would have adopted had he gotten into office, or whether a George Clinton-led ticket would have done better had he not been cut down by heart disease.

The Election of 1848

Politicians today thrive on a steady stream of poll results, while historically they appealed to popular acclaim. Decisions about issues both serious and mundane are usually based upon the opinion of the people, as perhaps they should be in a democracy. The decision to seek re-election or not is obviously heavily influenced by this factor. While such presidents as Woodrow Wilson, Harry Truman, and Lyndon Johnson could have run again for office, they declined to do so in part due to their crumbling poll numbers. It would be rare for a politician at the height of his or her popularity to actually decline to run again, yet this is precisely what happened in 1848.

James K. Polk had ridden into the White House as a dark horse candidate, a relative unknown outside his home state of North Carolina and in Washington political circles. He had famously promised to acquire an assortment of pieces of territory from Mexico and the United Kingdom, and also promised to lower the tariff rate. Additionally, Polk had pledged to do all of this in only one term, which at the time was undoubtedly a political ploy. Once in office, the new president not only fulfilled his promises but exceeded them as well. With a successful war with Mexico completed, the border of Oregon Territory peacefully settled, California acquired, and the tariff lowered, the majority of Americans genuinely loved Polk. Despite this he chose not to run again for election in 1848.

Polk, though the youngest president elected up until that time, had grown older and sicker over the course of his four years in office. In his diary he began to express both his dissatisfaction with the office of the presidency and his fears about his generally poor health. In one entry in April 1848, Polk wrote of his hopes to complete a book on his time in office, ". . . if a kind providence permits me length of days and health."[249] Though the Democratic Party implored him to run, sending various sen-

A PESTILENCE ON PENNSYLVANIA AVENUE

ators to the White House in late 1847 and early 1848, he declined in part
due to his health concerns. Polk's aggressively hands-on approach to the
Mexican War contributed to the destruction of his already frail constitution.

Without Polk as a candidate, the Democratic Party settled on Senator Lewis Cass. Though a general during the War of 1812, he lacked the
military pedigree and renown of his Whig opponent, General Zachary
Taylor. Worse yet, Cass's pro-slavery leanings split the Democratic convention and led to the organization of the Free Soil Party under Martin
Van Buren. This schism would shatter previously secure political holds on
a variety of counties and states and ultimately throw New York and its
thirty-six electoral votes to Taylor. Though it remains an unknown if Polk
could have held the party together, Cass certainly could not.

As Polk and his wife began their month-long journey home in
March 1849, he was already quite ill with "a derangement of the stomach
and bowels."[250] Since diarrhea had plagued him his entire presidency, he
seems to not have taken the episode too seriously, and even thought that
the condition would help to protect him from the cholera then ravaging
the Deep South.[251] As an added precaution, Polk also quarantined himself,
arguing, "During the prevalence of cholera I deem it prudent to remain
as much as possible at my own house."[252] Yet despite this sound precaution, only 103 days after leaving the White House, Polk was dead. While
various theories abound as to the exact nature of his illness, cholera tends
to be the widely accepted cause. Had Polk been re-elected, his possible
death while in office would have propelled his vice president into the
White House. It is doubtful that George Dallas would have continued in
this role due to his stand on the Walker Tariff and several other issues that
crippled his support in Pennsylvania. Whoever the party may have chosen
as the new vice president would have certainly been the next president as
well. Instead the Whigs moved into power and promptly put a halt to the
Manifest Destiny ideology of President Polk.

The Election of 1872

Ulysses S. Grant was a gifted general and war hero who proved to be a
less-than-competent president. His first few years in office, though not

without economic or foreign policy successes, were beset with scandals and administrative failings. Anger over these actions, when combined with a growing sense of dissatisfaction with Reconstruction, led to the creation of the Liberal Republican Party in 1872. As a result, two separate Republican conventions were held that year to select candidates for the presidency. To many observers at the time it seemed that Grant's chances of securing a second term were fleeting at best.

At a convention in Cincinnati in May, the new party chose famed New York Tribune editor Horace Greeley as its candidate. Though he had only four months of legislative experience, his managerial skills, legions of devoted readers, and vitriolic tongue seemed adequate compensation. Greeley's platform of civil service reform and an end to Reconstruction quickly caught on with both northern and southern voters. In an odd twist, the Democratic Party, seeing this as their only chance to topple Grant and the Republicans, decided likewise to nominate Greeley at their July convention in Baltimore.

The concept of two political parties nominating the same individual was extremely rare in American politics in the nineteenth century, yet what Greeley did next was even rarer. Presidential candidates of the time did not actively run for president; the idea of a politician going out and begging for votes was seen as unseemly or pure demagoguery. Breaking with tradition, Greeley immediately took to the back roads and cities of the nation, delivering speech after speech in order to garner support. His thrilling stump discourses attracted ever-growing crowds and overshadowed the addresses of Grant's vice president and others. Despite receiving massive financial support from the richest men and businesses of the day, Grant's cause appeared doomed.

What allowed the president to keep his office were a series of illnesses that struck Greeley and his family. In June 1872, Mary Young (Cheney) Greeley, the wife of the Democratic presidential candidate, fell gravely ill after returning home from Europe. Her sickness slowed the pace of the campaign and allowed the Republicans to regain ground in the competition. By October, her condition had worsened and her husband called a stop to his campaigning altogether. When Mary died on October 30 of the tuberculosis that had affected her for years, her husband fell into a deep despair from which he never fully recovered. A week later Grant was re-elected in a landslide, winning thirty-one states to Greeley's six. The Democratic candidate himself died three weeks later on November 29, having exhausted himself during the campaign. If he had won, Radical Republican Benjamin Gratz Brown would have been president instead. The latter had his own personal issues, becoming so notoriously drunk at a campaign picnic that he attempted to butter a watermelon.

The Election of 1884

Although most Americans largely forget Chester A. Arthur, he was quite popular while in office. As already discussed, Arthur's Bright's disease was slowly killing him. By the time of the 1884 Republican National Convention in Chicago, he had firmly decided against running for a second term. He had only recently returned from a trip to Florida, which had only further enervated him, and certainly knew by this point that his disease was fatal. The White House doctor recorded as early as 1882 that the president was "sick in body and soul."[253]

Even with only a lackluster interest in the nomination, Arthur still polled a close second to the eventual candidate James G. Blaine, who required four ballots to finally secure the candidacy. The Democrats chose Grover Cleveland, a much less-well-known figure than Blaine. Due to accusations of Blaine's personal corruption and the notorious "rum, Romanism, and rebellion" comment delivered by one of his supporters, the Republican candidate lost the state of New York by only 1,149 votes. Cleveland squeaked by with a 219 to 182 electoral vote win and a popular margin of only 58,000. While Arthur would not have survived a second term, dying as he did in November 1886, his personal stature in New York, combined with his general popularity, would most likely have won him the state and therefore the election. Instead his fatal illness helped to break the quarter-century Republican grip on the White House.

The Elections of 1912 and 1920

Rarely does a politician who removes themselves from politics successfully reenter the arena. Electability depends on recognition and accomplishment, two criteria that are often lost when someone vacates the playing field for the stands. Yet if any man could do so it would be Theodore Roosevelt. The famed Bull Mouse had battled illness and disease his entire life, a constant war that helped mold and inspire his unique political philosophy. His varied illnesses and injuries included severe asthma, terrible myopia, blindness in one eye from a boxing match, a gunshot wound to his chest, otitis media, and malaria. Yet all of these maladies did not keep him from running or considering running for the office of president at least three times.

After almost eight years in the White House, during which he helped to push the nation towards Progressivism, Theodore Roosevelt stepped down in 1909. He handpicked William Howard Taft to replace him, and afterwards busied himself with a yearlong scientific safari to Africa. Though he kept himself occupied by killing or collecting some 11,000 insects and animals, he also kept an eager eye on politics back home. Roosevelt soon grew disenchanted with Taft, judging him to have betrayed the torch of Progressivism that he had passed on.

Taft had never truly desired to be president. But when Roosevelt announced his attentions to claim the nomination in 1912, Taft stubbornly decided to hold on to power. Teddy ran an amazing grass roots campaign, securing votes of confidence from many states in the primitive primary system of the day. However, Taft maintained control of the party machine itself and secured the Republican nomination in Chicago in June. Undaunted, Roosevelt and his supporters stormed out of the hall and formed the rival Progressive Party across town, claiming Taft had the "brains of a guinea pig."

Roosevelt's decision merely served to split the Republican vote and throw the election towards Woodrow Wilson. In fact the Democratic candidate secured fewer votes than did the previous candidates in 1908, 1900, or 1896. Yet all of this could have changed had it not been for Roosevelt's terrible myopia and associated eye damage. On October 14, 1912, only a few weeks before the general election, Roosevelt was in Milwaukee to make a last-minute appeal to the Progressives of the region. As the crowd cheered, the former president stood up in his car to acknowledge them and at that moment was shot in the chest during an attempted assassination. His assailant was John Schrank, an unemployed man who had stalked the former president from Louisiana to Wisconsin. Schrank's apparent motive seems to have been his opposition to Roosevelt's potential violation of the third term principle.[254]

Despite Roosevelt's declaration that "it takes more than that to kill a bull moose," it was really not his strength and bravado that saved him. Within his army coat chest pocket was his folded, fifty-page speech and his steel eyeglass case. The assassin's .38 caliber bullet tore through the speech, hit the case, and was slowed enough to only just barely penetrate Teddy's chest. The bullet lodged in one of his ribs, where it would remain for the rest of his life. Roosevelt spoke for more than an hour before he went to the hospital. Thanks to his terrible vision and eye injury, his life was spared. Had the former president been killed, it is questionable whether the Progressive ticket would have continued without him or whether his running mate Hiram Johnson could have garnered many votes. The Republican breach might have been mended and Wilson's victory and all that was to follow might never have occurred.

Teddy Roosevelt had hopes to run again for the presidency in 1920. After eight years of Wilson, including the latter's personal efforts to ruin Roosevelt's plans to form an all-volunteer unit to take to Europe during the Great War, the old Bull Moose decided to come out of retirement. At just over sixty years of age, he felt that he was still young enough to handle the hardships of national office. As early as 1918, he began giving speeches to help the Republicans retake Congress and boost his own chances for nomination. Yet his reoccurring malaria was beginning to take a toll, and he was forced to step aside in favor of another candidate. Their choice was General Leonard Wood, one of Roosevelt's old companions. Though Wood initially led in the 1920 Republican convention in Chicago, by the ninth ballot he was being edged out by Warren G. Harding, a representative of the more conservative Taft wing of the party. Roosevelt had died unexpectedly in January 1919, and did not live to see his final defeat by Taft. Had Teddy lived, some historians are confident that he would have easily picked up the nomination and won in the general contest as well.[255] The politically conservative Roaring Twenties would have been a far different decade with the internationalist and Progressive Roosevelt at the helm.

The Election of 1960

The electoral contest that unfolded in 1960 between John F. Kennedy and Richard M. Nixon was unique for a number of reasons. The youth of the two men represented a generational shift from the previous administrations of Franklin Roosevelt, Harry Truman, and Ike. What was more important, however, was their approach to attracting votes from the general public. In an effort to employ the latest forms of communication, the men took to both radio and television to deliver their messages. However, the most memorable moments in the campaign for most were the televised debates between the two men.

The famed Sindlinger & Company surveys showed that while Nixon dominated those audiences who listened to the radio, Kennedy managed to edge him out among television viewers. Historically this has been taken to mean that Kennedy's looks and expressions of confidence impressed the public more than Nixon's experience and superior answers.

Yet it was not Kennedy's youthful appearance and tan that moved voters as much as Nixon's swarthier look, caused by a series of health issues. The vice president had just emerged from the hospital twelve days earlier after undergoing a knee operation for a serious staphylococcal infection; Nixon looked sickly and had lost a considerable amount of weight. His subsequent decision to launch a three-day, fourteen-state blitz further wore away at him. On the night of the first debate, viewers saw a pale-faced man with a five o'clock shadow, whose shirt was at least a size too large due to weight loss associated with his illness. Finally, when exiting his Buick to enter CBS studios in New York City, Nixon banged his knee on the car door, further aggravating his recent wound. His pained expression and clear favoring of the other leg tended to produce an awkward presence on stage.[256] Interestingly, Kennedy's tan appearance had less to do with his careful cosmetic preparation for the debate and more to with a visible side effect of his Addison's disease.

In addition, due to Mamie Eisenhower's concern for her husband's health, the Nixon campaign did not schedule him for any appearances in the final few weeks of the election. When combined with his previous flippant answers to questions from reporters regarding Vice President Nixon's accomplishments, this absence certainly did not help to sway voters. In the end Richard Nixon's health issues and some questionable polling place results helped to usher Kennedy into the White House.

The Election of 1968

Lyndon Baines Johnson faced a similar situation to Chester Arthur and Woodrow Wilson with regard to his re-election in 1968. Though he felt he was personally still popular in the Democratic Party, the issue of Vietnam was slowly eating away at his presidency. More important as a determining factor for Johnson was his health. LBJ had experienced several heart attacks in the 1950s and 1960s and had fears of a fatal one. As his chief of staff recounted twenty years later, "He talked about his health and repeated that his father and grandfather had died of heart failure at age 64. He said that he could not complete another full term as president, since he would be 64 during the last year of that term."[257] Johnson appeared on national television in March 1968 and announced his decision to not seek another term as president. Johnson lived another four years, and died unexpectedly in his bed in 1973. He was sixty-four.

The Elections of 1972 and 1988

The advent and popularization of modern psychology eventually brought mental health into the realm of politics. While the emotional state of previous presidents and presidential candidates can certainly be debated, proof of such issues has only recently been available. Not surprisingly, these topics soon became matters of intense interest for opposition candidates.

The earliest case of this was during the 1972 election. President Nixon was quite popular at the time, having presided over a drawdown in the Vietnam War and a lessening of the violent tensions and riots of the 1960s. His opponent, George McGovern, secured the Democratic nomination thanks in part to an aggressive grassroots campaign. But the party was far from enthusiastic about a candidate who was perceived as quite radical by many within his own circle. McGovern was famously dubbed the "Amnesty, Abortion, and Acid" candidate, a label that stuck for years.[258]

Not surprisingly, the vice presidential vote also proved to be bedlam, with seventy-nine names being thrown into the mix. In the end Senator Thomas Eagleton of Missouri was nominated by a less than enthusiastic convention. Almost immediately upon his selection, Nixon's CREEP (Committee for the Re-election of the President) began to dig into the background of both men. On July 19, 1972, Sam Krupnick, a Nixon supporter from Missouri, wrote to the president's secretary to share that Eagleton was alleged to have spent time in the Malcolm Bliss Mental Hospital in St. Louis, Missouri. Though Krupnick offered "acute alcoholism" as a potential cause, the truth was actually far more damning to the McGovern campaign.[259]

Senator Eagleton had thrice checked himself into a mental hospital for depression in the 1960s. On two of these occasions he had undergone electroconvulsive shock therapy. The McGovern team was taken by surprise when these accusations began to surface. Eagleton had never been their first choice and had not been fully vetted prior to the convention's vote. Scrambling to perform damage control, Eagleton confronted the issue head-on. In an address two weeks later he told the public, "On three occasions in my life, I have voluntarily gone into hospitals as result of nervous exhaustion and fatigue."[260]

Though McGovern announced that he backed his running mate 1,000 percent, concerns soon began to surface. As his campaign manager and future presidential candidate Gary Hart of Colorado said, "This was the height of the Cold War. The key here wasn't how do we feel about mental illness or therapy or anything like that. The key was—finger on the button." Though a poll at the time showed 77 percent of Americans did not care too much about the issue, McGovern soon decided to drop his running mate as a candidate. Only eighteen days after his selection, Eagleton was off the ticket. In the end, though this certainly helped to damage McGovern as a viable candidate, it probably was only one contributing factor to his already flawed and failed campaign.

A similar scenario unfolded in 1988 during the George H.W. Bush-Michael Dukakis battle for the presidency. In August of that year outgoing president Ronald Reagan, when asked for a comment about Democratic candidate Dukakis, said he "... did not want to pick on an invalid."[261] The Democrats quickly began to flood the media with medical records of the candidate, hoping to counter an Eagleton moment. For several weeks various members of the Republican Party had hinted that Dukakis had been treated for depression after his brother's death. These rumors were only buttressed by the candidate's initial and bizarre refusal to release his medical records. Though the issue did not destroy his campaign, it added yet another element of doubt and suspicion to an already tottering run for the presidency.

The Election of 1992

Despite George H.W. Bush's crushing defeat of Michael Dukakis in 1988 and his success at waging the Persian Gulf War, an economic contraction began to eat away at his popularity by the time of his re-election campaign in 1992. Seeking to boost his faltering image, President Bush departed on a twelve-day photo op trip to Asia shortly after Christmas.

On January 9, 1992, after having spent the morning playing a strenuous tennis game against the emperor and crown prince of Japan, the sixty-seven-year-old president attended a dinner at Prime Minister Miyazawa's home. During the banquet, Bush suddenly began to vomit and then fainted, all of which was caught on camera. The embarrassing incident was quickly disseminated to every major television network around the world, producing both weeks of jokes as well as true concerns about the health of the elderly leader, especially when compared to the youth and vigor of Governor Bill Clinton.

The administration reported that the president was suffering from a mild case of influenza. With his own aged presidency coming so closely upon the heels of Reagan's, questions soon began to be raised. *The New York Times* couched its coverage with references to Bush's age, writing:

> Mr. Fitzwater said today that the President, who is 67 years old, required no medication beyond an anti-nausea drug, but that Mr. Bush still experienced 'some weakness' and that as a result, his morning schedule had been canceled. He said the President had a good night's sleep and would resume his schedule this afternoon. 'The doctors are certain that there is no other illness or any other problems related to this, that it's a simple case of the flu.' he said. 'The President is human; he gets sick.'[262]

Concern over the president's health also led to one of the most notorious hoaxes to hit twenty-four-hour news. On January 10, 1992, James Edward Smith, a seventy-one-year old from Idaho, called CNN. Identifying himself only as the president's personal physician, he announced that Bush had died only three hours after the vomiting incident. The anchor, Don Harrison, began to relate the story, believing it to be genuine, only to be stopped at the last second by a supervisor. Smith was later investigated by the Secret Service and soon after confined to a mental hospital. Presidential health concerns, when combined with the new medium of the twenty-four-hour news cycle, helped to further convince many Americans that Bush was simply too old for the job.

The president's re-election campaign was more irreparably harmed by the death of famed Republican strategist Lee Atwater. A prominent member of the two Reagan presidential campaigns, Atwater had helped to spearhead Bush's win in 1988, developing some of the most vicious and successful attacks against Dukakis. In recognition of his skill and devotion, Atwater was named chairman of the Republican National Committee in 1989 and almost immediately began to plan for Bush's re-election.

Just as the 1990 midterm election campaigns were taking off, Atwater collapsed at a fundraising event. He was soon diagnosed with a grade III astrocytoma, an aggressive and incurable brain cancer. Barely a year after this diagnosis he was dead. Many speculated at the time and since that had Atwater survived, Bush would have run a much more aggressive campaign in 1992, especially with all of the potential dirt available about then-Gov. Bill Clinton.[263]

The Elections of 1996 and 2008

Despite advances in medicine, with all of the connections between politics and disease it is hardly surprising that the potential of illness has also emerged as a campaign issue. The tendency of the Republican Party to run more aged candidates in comparison to the Democrats over the past sixty years has also resulted in this becoming a more one-sided issue. In fact out of the sixteen elections since 1952, the Republican candidate has been older than his adversary in thirteen instances. The average age of Democratic candidates is 52.5 years, while that of Republicans has been 62.6 years.

The two elections where age became a notable issue during the campaign were in 1996 and 2008. Both elections saw Republicans well-above 70 years of age running against Democrats who were 50 and 47 years old, respectively. In 1996, Senator Bob Dole was 73 years old when he took on Bill Clinton, a man 23 years his junior. His age almost immediately became a talking point, with commercials running as early as May describing his policies as "old." Clinton's supporters also employed loaded words and phrases such as "dysfunctional" and "worn-out rhetoric" as allusions to his perceived mental and physical feebleness.[264] Late night comics soon joined in, with David Letterman quipping, "a lot of people would look at a glass as half empty. Bob Dole looks at the glass and says, 'What a great place to put my teeth.'" All of this talk was based on some fact, as Bob Dole had been treated for prostate cancer only five years before, though apart from this he seemed to be in excellent health. Both men were quizzed about the age issue during a debate on October 16, with Dole attempting to both relate his age to wisdom as well as redirect the issue to Clinton's poor performance in the White House, saying "Well, I think age is very—you know, wisdom comes from age, experience and intelligence. And if you have some of each—and I have some age, some experience and some intelligence—that adds up to wisdom. I think it also is a strength. It's an advantage. And I have a lot of young people work in my office, work in my campaign."[265] At the same time Clinton attempted to transform the issue from one of Dole's age to the age of his ideas: "I can only tell you that I don't think Senator Dole is too old to be president. It's the age of his ideas that I question. You're almost not old enough to remember this. But we tried this before, promising people an election year tax cut that's not paid for."[266] Dole did little to help his cause while on the campaign trail, famously falling off of a stage during an event and mentioning the long-defunct Brooklyn Dodgers in a speech.

Clinton handily defeated Dole, who, surprisingly, lost even the elderly vote to the sitting president. Though polls taken before November showed that only 34 percent of Americans thought that Dole's age could be an impediment, that figure represents a substantial number of potentially lost votes. For now ageism remains an acceptable weapon in politics.

The Barack Obama-John McCain electoral battle of 2008 saw many of the same issues as Dole's campaign twelve years before. This time the Republican candidate was pitted against a man 25 years his junior. The 72-year-old McCain, despite his military heroism, years of legislative experience, acknowledged leadership capability, and moderate positions on many issues, was almost immediately assaulted for his age. CNN even went so far as to run an article in June 2008 with the opening salvo, "Is Sen. John McCain too old to be president?"[267] The clearly biased piece compared the then-current election to both 1996 and 1984 in an effort to bunch the various Republican septuagenarians together. Various Obama delegates and supporters questioned McCain's sanity and health, calling him "confused" and "out of touch." Democrats voraciously seized upon a pronouncement by the candidate himself stating that he was unable to use a computer, though McCain was merely referring to the injuries he sustained during the Vietnam War that limited the movement of his arms and fingers.[268]

The release of John McCain's health records became a talking points issue during the campaign, with many speculating that the Republican candidate had something to hide. The majority of this concern resolved around his bout with melanoma in 2000. Various newspapers began requesting access to the documents as early as March 2008, well before the actual convention of either party was held.[269] To help head off further speculation, McCain released all of his records in May of that year. To his credit, the candidate had previously released 1,500 pages of medical information in 1999, during his first run for the presidency, perhaps the greatest trove of political health documents ever to be given to the American public.

Not surprisingly, while professing concerns about McCain's advanced age, few media outlets turned as much negative attention to Obama's extreme youth. Though the Democrats released their candidate's health records shortly after Republicans did, it was merely a short, undated summary by a physician. In addition, the letter glossed over the candidate's smoking habit and contained a bizarre reference to his "good intake of roughage and fluids."

McCain's advanced age weighed upon the thoughts of many voters and was one of the prime factors in his decision to adopt a much younger running mate. His thoroughness in releasing more than 1,500 pages of medical information perhaps merely magnified the issue in the public's eyes. In the end, though the election was not decided by age or health concerns, these stories perhaps distracted some voters from the true issues.

Chapter 10

SECOND IN LINE, FIRST IN HEALTH

"I have received my mortal blow; but I greatly desire to
remain a few years longer to finish my work."
(Henry Wilson, 1875)

The office of vice president constitutionally involves few duties.
Arguably the most important has been to succeed the president
upon his death and maintain the continuity of government in the nation. Because of this the health of the vice president has been of interest
historically, as was seen with Franklin Roosevelt's choice of a running
mate in 1944 and John McCain's in 2008. On several occasions, the
illness or death of vice presidents has helped to alter the path of the
republic, or at least provide for interesting politics.

The administration of James Madison was important for a number
of reasons, with perhaps the most significant being the War of 1812.
Yet it also bears the distinctions of seeing not only the first death of a
sitting vice president, but of the second as well. Following the political
disgrace of Aaron Burr, Jefferson removed him from the ticket in 1804.
Still desiring to win New York for the Republican Party, the president
soon settled on Governor George Clinton of that state as his running
mate. Vice President Clinton remained the party's number two man in
the 1808 election as well, again carrying his home state, but this time
for James Madison. Clinton seemed intent on running for a third term,
despite his political conflicts with, and personal misgivings about, James

Madison, when he experienced a sudden heart attack on April 20, 1812. Clinton's heavily mourned death removed a potential challenge to the Virginia dominance of the presidency.

In keeping with the Virginia-New York ticket that had served the Republicans well since 1800, Madison again searched for a running mate from the Empire State in 1812. This selection was all the more important as the raging War of 1812 was proving to be unpopular with New Englanders, a situation which threatened to cost Jefferson's party the White House. Madison chose Governor Elbridge Gerry of Massachusetts, who was in financial trouble following his recent loss of power in Boston, to be his next vice president. Though Gerry failed to deliver either his home state or New York to Madison, the two men were still elected. Gerry went on to famously use his power to help arrest and investigate New England Federalists. Luckily for his opponents, he was taken ill during the summer of 1813, most likely having suffered a stroke. On November 23, 1814, he was struck ill again and died in the capital. As one author put it, "A sudden extravasation of blood took place upon the lungs and terminated his life within twenty minutes."[270] The country would not have a second-in-command until 1817.

The election of James Monroe in 1816 helped to usher in both the Era of Good Feelings and a new vice president. Daniel Tompkins was a successful war governor from New York who had helped to organize the state's efforts against the British. When the Federalist-heavy state assembly was reluctant to fund the various expeditions during the War of 1812, Tompkins personally paid for the soldiers and equipment. In fact, the majority of his time in office as vice president was spent attempting to secure repayment of the estimated $120,000 that he was personally owed.

Tompkins's financial struggles, combined with a terrible riding accident suffered early in his term, severely restricted his activities. He was absent from his post at least three-fourths of the time and soon after turned to alcohol.[271] In fact, "he was several times so drunk in the chair that he could [only] with difficulty put the question."[272] His drunken episodes soon aroused the concern of many of those around him. Upon stepping down from the vice presidency in March 1825, Tompkins returned to New York, and ninety-nine days after leaving office he was dead.

The shortest term for a vice president belongs to William Rufus King of Alabama. Infamous for his alleged homosexual relationship with future president James Buchanan, King was second in line to the presidency more than once. In 1850, following the death of Zachary Taylor and the ascension of Millard Fillmore, King, as president *pro tempore* of the Senate, was next in line to the presidency should Fillmore also die. Two years later, in 1852, he was Franklin Pierce's running mate. By this time, King was had contracted tuberculosis and was near death.

Believed to have acquired the illness while serving as minister to France between 1844 and 1846, King was selected solely to appease the Buchanan wing of the party. Pierce himself confided to a friend that his running mate was "Buchanan's bosom buddy." Despite his illness, Buchanan endeavored to ensure Southern support for the Yankee Pierce, claiming Pierce was a "northern man with southern principles." In January 1853, shortly after their victory, King traveled to Cuba, hoping that the climate there would be less favorable to his consumption. He wrote in December, "My health is not good. I am troubled by a distressing cough."[273] A special act of Congress was passed to allow him to take the oath of office on March 24, 1853, after which he returned to his native Alabama. Little more than three weeks later, on April 18, he died, never once having presided over the Senate.

Above all else, throughout his time in office Abraham Lincoln strived to unite the fragmented nation. In keeping with this, he chose a Democrat, Andrew Johnson, to be his running mate in 1864, after dumping Hannibal Hamlin of Maine. This National Union ticket, as it was called, was intended to symbolize the casting aside of partisan differences in favor of a united front against the Confederacy. Although Johnson was well-known to many and had remained loyal to the Union throughout the war, a bout with typhoid fever almost cost him his new position.

As also happened to 79,000 soldiers during the war, newly elected Vice President Andrew Johnson was stricken with typhoid over the winter of 1864–1865. Finding it difficult to shake the disease, he remained ill during his inauguration in March 1865. To steady his condition, Johnson consumed three whiskeys in Hamlin's office and afterward made a spectacle of himself on the Senate floor. As recounted by Senator Zachariah Chandler, "The inauguration went off very well except that the Vice President Elect was too drunk to perform his duties and disgraced himself and the Senate by making a drunken foolish speech. I was never so mortified in my life, had I been able to find a hole I would have dropped through it out of sight." Outraged Radical Republicans went so far as to draft a resolution to Lincoln demanding Johnson's resignation, and some even pushed for impeachment. The rumors of Johnson's alcoholism would dog him for years, and impact his future presidency along the way. In reality it was the typhoid bacterium that was to blame. Had Johnson been removed from office or had he succumbed to the illness like so many others during the war, Senate President Pro Tempore Lafayette S. Foster of Connecticut would have become the next leader of the nation. Foster incidentally would have also risen to the post had John Wilkes Booth's fellow conspirators succeeded in killing the vice president as well as the president.

Due largely to his appeal to Radical Republicans, Henry Wilson of Massachusetts was chosen to replace Schuyler Colfax as President U.S. Grant's running mate in 1872. Thanks in part to Horace Greeley's death, Grant handily won re-election. Apart from suggestions that he had received bribes as part of the Credit Mobilier scandal, Wilson's time in office was largely uneventful. The general domestic peace within the nation allowed him to devote most of his time toward completing his great historical work, *The Rise and Fall of the Slave-Power in America.*

Wilson's health soon began to fail, and he suffered a stroke in 1873. This attack left his face partially paralyzed and forced him to take a reprieve for the summer in Natick, Massachusetts. A servant girl told any visitors to the house who inquired about the vice president there was only "an invalid stopping here."[274] By 1874, he had recovered enough to preside over the opening of the Senate, but this brief revitalization proved to be fleeting. In the fall of 1875, while attending a convention at Young's Hotel in Boston, he was stricken with another paralytic attack and suffered more damage to his face and his ability to speak. He understood that his time was limited, stating, "I have received my mortal blow; but I greatly desire to remain a few years longer to finish my work."[275] He struggled to recover, and on November 10, 1875, after suffering another attack while bathing in the new Italian marble bathtubs that had been installed in the basement of the Capitol, he was carried to his room in the Senate. On November 22 he passed away in his office. An autopsy revealed the presence of almost fifty ounces of blood in his brain sinus.[276]

With the various cover-ups regarding presidential health, it was only a matter of time before a vice presidential candidate attempted the same scheme. Except for the ascension to office of Andrew Johnson under tragic conditions, by 1884 Republicans had dominated the White House for twenty-four years. Over the course of this time in power, issues of corruption and the Long Depression had begun to weigh down on the Grand Old Party. To capitalize on their chances, Democrats nominated the sitting governor of New York, Grover Cleveland. A moderate reformer and hard-money man with no connection to the Civil War, "Grover the Good" could appeal to various factions of both the Democratic and Republican parties. To further secure the election, the party felt that a running mate from a Midwestern state would help to steal additional states from the Republicans. As this was, in essence, the same strategy that was employed during the almost successful election of 1876, many argued for the same running mate, Thomas Hendricks.

The former governor of Indiana, Hendricks had unsuccessfully run with Samuel Tilden in 1876 before being deprived of their win with the Compromise of 1877. He was then selected to run again in 1880, but turned down the offer in part due to his poor health and in part due to not being nominated for the presidency, which he thought was his due. However, 1884 was his last chance at gaining higher office. Hendricks had suffered two strokes, one shortly after the election of 1880 while visiting Hot Springs, Arkansas, and one in 1882. The first attack produced partial paralysis in his right arm, while the second left him unable to walk for any extended amount of time. Hendricks kept his condition quiet and no one outside of his immediate family and doctor knew of his lameness. [277] His eagerness to accept the nomination probably had less to do with his support of Cleveland, a man whom he had never met, and more to do with his desire to end his life at the head of the Senate.

Despite some scandalous accusations against Cleveland, the Democrats carried both New York and Indiana, as predicted, and carried the election. Friction soon developed between the two men since Cleveland rarely if ever consulted Hendricks, or even called him into the White House. Hendricks told reporters, "I have not seen the President in four months."[278] Any tension was short lived and left no scars on

Cleveland's presidency, since on November 25, 1885, Vice President Hendricks died in his sleep while on a trip to Indianapolis.

Perhaps the greatest episodes of vice presidential illness influencing the path of American history concerned two of the larger-than-life men to hold the office. The first of these, Garret Hobart of New Jersey, rose to power with William McKinley in the election of 1896. As opposed to previous political pairings, Hobart was chosen for his similarities to McKinley rather than his differences. Perhaps his only salient addition to the ticket was the state of New Jersey and its ten electoral votes. The state had historically been staunchly Democratic, having only gone Republican once, in 1872, following the untimely death of Horace Greeley. Thanks to the skill and talents of both men, the Republicans won the election, even carrying the Garden State in the process.

Garret Hobart proved to be a popular and successful vice president. In the Senate he was well-respected and helped to champion much of the president's platform. His two most important moments arose with the advent of the Spanish American War. Even after years of yellow journalism, the publication of the De Lome letter, and the sinking of the USS *Maine*, McKinley was still reluctant to go to war. Hobart became one of the driving forces behind the president's ultimate decision to do so, confiding, "Mr. President, I can no longer hold back the Senate. They will act without you if you do not act at once." Following the successful conclusion of the war, he cast his only tie-breaking vote in favor of securing the Philippines for America, thus helping to begin the nation's brief flirtation with imperialism and putting in motion a chain of events that would eventually see the nation enter World War II.

Unfortunately Hobart's health began to fail him shortly after the declaration of war. He became afflicted with heart disease and soon experienced occasional fainting spells. In addition he seems to have suffered a heart attack at some point before the Senate adjourned for the winter of 1898-1899. The true extent of his condition was kept from the American people but not from McKinley. Demonstrating the closeness between the two men, the president brought the sickened vice president with him to Thomasville, Georgia, for the winter. While there, Hobart contracted the flu for the second time in a year, which seems to have only exacerbated his condition. Though McKinley publically insisted that Hobart would remain on the ticket for the 1900 election, he was inwardly concerned. The two men summered in 1899 on Lake Champlain, but Hobart spent much of the time in bed. Upon his return, McKinley wrote to him to inquire as to his health.[279] After spending some time at the Jersey Shore, the vice president returned to his home in Paterson, New Jersey, where he grew so weak that he was forced to sleep in a chair for comfort, a classic sign of congestive heart failure. He would remain away from the Senate and in his home until his death on November 21, 1899.

The true importance of Hobart has been argued to be his death, which helped to push Theodore Roosevelt into the vice presidency, and ultimately the White House, following McKinley's assassination. Historian Michael J. Connolly perhaps best sums up a Hobart presidency had he survived:

A Hobart Administration would have tightly allied with Old Guard Republicanism…as opposed to Teddy Roosevelt's hyper-active progressivism. High tariffs would protect US factories and the gold standard defended from popular upstarts like Bryan. He would have been the railroad industry's advocate, opposing any further regulation (like the 1906 Hepburn Act), and resisted anti-trust attacks. He would have weakened the ICC and appointed Supreme Court justices who would have backed the Joint Traffic Association. While he loyally supported 1890s American colonial expansion, Hobart lacked McKinley's messianic, Christianizing, "civilizing" impulse and would have steered a frugal, insular, restrained foreign policy. President Hobart would not have intervened in the Russo-Japanese War, sent the Great White Fleet around the world, or grabbed land for the Panama Canal…Progressivism would have been temporarily derailed.[280]

The health of the vice president continued to be a topic for concern well into the twentieth century. James Sherman, Taft's vice president, was the last holder of that office to die while in power, succumbing to Bright's Disease in 1912. A generation later, concern was expressed over the mental health of Henry A. Wallace, and still later the constant health issues confronting Richard Cheney become popular fodder for the media. With so much power and potential influence, a vice president's diseases and illnesses are often of as much importance as those of the president.

Chapter 11

ILLNESSES OF THE FIRST LADIES

"I think the doctors would especially like to keep one in bed.
The love of money is the root of all evil."
(Mary Todd Lincoln, 1870)

The position of first lady was not envisioned by the Founding Fathers, but instead evolved organically during the course of the republic's history. As with many other institutions of this type, it has proven to be all the more stronger and effective because of its unforced development. The role of the first lady has itself changed from the days of Martha Washington to its present holder, from a matron hostess to a campaigner for specific causes. Due to this influence on both the nation and their husbands, it is not surprising to find that the health and illnesses of these women have often been important matters. Far from being simply a family affair, their importance has entered even mainstream politics.

Martha Washington

The first woman to hold the position of first lady, Martha Dandridge Washington, left her mark on the nation for a variety of reasons. In terms of her health, her importance began with an event that preceded her husband's time in office. During the early days of the Revolution, Washington and most other commanders were concerned with the potential dangers of an outbreak of smallpox among the gathered colonial soldiers. As was recounted in Chapter One, General Washington became a vocal proponent of inoculation among his soldiers by 1776. Yet some authors claim that Martha's decision to be inoculated herself was the impetus needed to push a reluctant George into undertaking the campaign.[281] The idea of the general's wife being protected against the notorious illness, but not his soldiers, would have been difficult to explain to the public, the army, or Congress.

By the time her husband became president, Martha was a mature woman who had filled out over the years. She is reported to have suffered from colic and severe stomach pains and often had to consult a physician. After their final return to Mount Vernon in 1797, she appears to have suffered several bouts of malaria, and so was treated with quinine. Martha Washington would outlive her husband by only two years. Stricken with dementia, she perished in 1802 at the age of seventy.

Martha Skelton Jefferson

Martha Skelton Randolph, the wife of Thomas Jefferson, never lived to see the White House, but her early death helped to launch one of the most notorious of early political scandals. Born Martha Wayles, she married her first husband, Bathurst Skelton, in 1766. Less than two years later, her husband was dead and she was a widow with a young child. Shortly after the death of her first husband, Martha began a relationship with Thomas Jefferson and the couple married just over two years later on January 1, 1772. The marriage seems to have been a loving one as evidenced by his tender caring for her during her frequent illnesses. As recorded by his daughter Patsy Jefferson, "He nursed my poor mother in turn with Aunt Carr and her own sister—sitting up with her and administering her medicines and drink to the last. For four months that she lingered he was never out of calling. When not at her bedside, he was writing in a small room which opened immediately at the head of her bed."[282] Martha became pregnant at least seven times, with each incident impacting her health more and more. By the time of her last pregnancy in 1782, she became frail and was confined to her bed. In September 1782, four months after giving birth, she passed away. Jefferson was inconsolable for weeks, again demonstrating the affection between the two. Upon her deathbed, Martha had asked Thomas never to marry again, and this was a promise he would keep for the remainder of his life.

Although Jefferson was a man of his word, he was also a man with emotional and physical needs. Only two years after the death of his wife, the Continental Congress appointed him the nation's envoy to France. Accompanying him was a young slave girl, Sally Hemings, with whom he allegedly began a decades-long affair. This was not uncommon at the time; his father-in-law had carried on just such a relationship, and had fathered Sally in 1773. Yet commonality did not translate into general acceptance. The Jefferson-Hemings affair became political fodder in the late 1790s and permeated all aspects of the election of 1800. Though it did not cost him his hard fought victory, it permanently impacted Jefferson's legacy. It is questionable that the devoted Jefferson would have undertaken the tryst had Martha Skelton survived.

Dolley Madison

One of the most influential of the early first ladies was Dolley Madison, famous for both her social skills while in the White House and her dramatic rescue of artifacts from the presidential mansion during the War of 1812. All of this would not have occurred if it had not been for a virulent outbreak of yellow fever in 1793. Born Dolley Payne in 1768, her Quaker family had migrated from North Carolina to Philadelphia at the start of Washington's presidency. After settling into the local society, she married Quaker lawyer John Todd in 1790. The marriage was fruitful and she gave birth to two sons in quick succession. Tragedy struck in 1793, when a massive yellow fever epidemic ravaged Philadelphia. More than 5,000 residents died, including John Todd and their second son, William.

Widowed at a young age, and with a small son to support, Dolley was fortunate to be introduced to a forty-three-year-old representative from Virginia and perpetual bachelor named James Madison. After the two were married in 1794 Dolley quickly became an active member of Washington society, and upon the election of the widowed Jefferson, served as something of an unofficial hostess for him. With her husband's own election in 1808, she began to play an even larger role in the expansion and care of the White House.

Dolley's most prominent contribution to the position of first lady was her foray into the social scene of the capital. She became the first presidential wife to relish and expand the role of the first lady by hosting parties, and representing her husband in society. Dolley Madison appeared on magazine covers, served as a fashion icon with her famous turbans, and even started a public project. Many subsequent first ladies would copy the latter action. Legends also persist that she was the first to serve ice cream at the White House, that she began the annual egg-rolling contest, and that she encouraged Francis Scott Key to board a British warship at the Battle of Fort McHenry, and thus set the stage for the writing of the "Star Spangled Banner."

Possibly her most famous action, and one that may be equally as apocryphal, was her rescuing of important artifacts from the White House as the British army approached to burn it in 1814. Though the American army had held out at Fort McHenry and driven the British away from Baltimore, a *chevauchee* of English soldiers headed for the new American capital with an aim to reduce it to ashes. President Madison was ferried to safety, but Dolley chose to stay behind, allegedly overseeing the removal of various invaluable artifacts and documents, including artist Gilbert Stuart's famed portrait of George Washington. She described her actions and thoughts to her sister, writing, "I confess that I was so unfeminine as to be free from fear, and willing to remain in the Castle! If I could have had a cannon through every window . . . my whole heart mourned for my country!"[283] Upon her return, she undertook the rebuilding, redecorating, and restocking of the once magnificent building. None of this would have been possible without the yellow fever-induced death of her first husband.

Rachel Jackson

The frontier region of Tennessee in the years after the Revolution was an area of adventure, opportunity, and occasional violence. It was here that Rachel Donelson grew into maturity and married Captain Lewis Robards, a local land speculator. However the differences between them were too great and after three years together they separated in the summer of 1788. Frontier law and civil procedure were often as vague as the boundaries of the new territory, and the two were not officially divorced.

Only three years later, Rachel fell in love with a young solicitor named Andrew Jackson. The two were soon married, but as Rachel Donelson's first marriage had never been annulled she was quickly accused of bigamy. A nasty divorce battle followed, which was not fully settled until 1794, at which point Andrew and Rachel remarried. The episode would have been of little historical interest had it not been picked up by John Quincy Adams' supporters in the election of 1828. The already vitriolic campaign turned especially disagreeable when Rachel Jackson's past marital issues came to light.

Attacks against Rachel for her technical polyandry proved to be the hardest accusations for Jackson to face. Rachel died unexpectedly on December 22, 1828, only a month after the election. The new president blamed Adams, saying, "May God Almighty forgive her murderers, as I know she forgave them. I never can."[284] Based upon her husband's descriptions of the pains she felt in her arms immediately preceding her death, it appears that Rachel died of a massive heart attack. Her untimely death, which was heavily mourned by Jackson, resulted in her niece, Emily Tennessee Donelson, becoming the unofficial hostess for the White House.

Emily Donelson's tenure as first lady by proxy was short lived. The Petticoat Affair, which centered on an alleged premarital affair between Peggy O'Neill and her new husband, Secretary of War John Henry Eaton, erupted in Washington in 1830 and threatened to derail Jackson's presidency. President Jackson took an unexpected interest in the scandal, and came to Mrs. Eaton's defense, largely due to what he saw as a repeat of history with the death of his own beloved wife. His niece, much like the majority of cabinet wives, refused to associate with the new Mrs. Eaton and returned home in the summer of 1830. This decision was most likely also necessitated by her ongoing battle with tuberculosis, a disease that would claim her life only six years later. Jackson eventually demanded the resignation of the majority of his cabinet, with the entire episode leading to a rift between him and Vice President John C. Calhoun.

For a number of reasons, not the least of which was the Petticoat Affair, Calhoun was removed from the Democratic ticket during the election of 1832, and Jackson chose Martin Van Buren to fill his place. The latter, though also forced to resign as per the president's request, had remained loyal to Jackson throughout the scandal. This began the rise to power of Van Buren and his northern branch of the Democratic

Party, a rise that would see him in the presidency four years later, and his branch of the party ascendant for a generation.

Other First Ladies

Though not every first lady experienced an illness that dramatically affected the path of the nation, their various health issues were nonetheless of some consequence to them and their husbands. Abigail Adams, for instance, was in perennially poor health, spending ever more time at their home in Quincy, Massachusetts, rather than in Washington, especially during her husband's time as vice president. Years later, Abigail advised her son to seek a milder climate to avoid the miasma of the capital.[285]

Many first ladies suffered from the effects of repeated childbirths, just as did many other women of the era. Elizabeth Monroe had her health broken following the birth and subsequent death of her first son from whooping cough in 1800. Though she recovered, she would experience a variety of other illnesses over the next few years. For instance, she appears to have suffered from epilepsy, once falling into an open fire in the White House during one of her attacks. Mrs. Monroe's various illnesses served to limit her social interactions, a contrast to Dolley Madison's frenetic social gatherings.

Louisa Adams, the wife of John Quincy Adams, likewise experienced a number of miscarriages during her fifty-year marriage. She also seems to have suffered from migraines and fainting spells, and was generally in poor health. Many of her ailments and complaints seem to speak of a slight mental illness, one with which the stoic Adamses were unsuited to deal. Louisa even referred to herself as "a maudlin hysterical fine Lady," a far cry from the legendary composure of her mother-in-law Abigail Adams.[286] While in Russia during her husband's tenure as minister to that nation, Louisa lost a child to dysentery and she herself was stricken with erysipelas. These further health issues deepened the strain in her relationship with John Quincy Adams. The low point in both her health and her marriage came during her husband's time in the White House. It seems that the onset of menopause substantially affected her mental and emotional health to the point where the two Adams were not communicating and were even taking separate vacations.[287]

Letitia Christian Tyler, the wife of John Tyler, served no role as first lady. Having suffered a debilitating stroke in 1839 shortly before the wedding of her son Robert, she was stricken as an invalid for the rest of her life. The symptoms expressed by Letitia prior to and following her stroke and as recorded by her family and friends seem to hint at hypertension as the cause of her condition.[288] Her time in the White House was largely spent confined to her bedroom as her husband waged political battles following his ascendency to office after the early death of William Henry Harrison. Though she did manage to appear downstairs for the marriage of her daughter in early 1842, this was most likely one of her only social appearances. After suffering a second stroke in the summer of that year she died in September, becoming the earliest first lady to die in office. The president's daughter-in-law Priscilla Cooper Tyler served as hostess for the next two years until John Tyler remarried a woman thirty years his junior in 1844, in a hurried ceremony in New York City. Tyler and his new wife, Julia Gardiner, met during a White House reception in 1842, and had begun a romance only a few months after his wife's death. These details, as well as the hushed ceremony, helped to create an atmosphere of scandal and gossip in the nation and led to an angry schism within Tyler's immediate family. Tyler himself was ecstatic, and the newlyweds left for a month-long honeymoon to Rip Raps, the site of President Jackson's old summer White House.

In a similar vein to Letitia Tyler, Abigail Powers Fillmore also remained inactive as first lady, largely due to an illness that she had suffered early in life. In July 1842, while departing from Washington, Abigail sprained her ankle, twisting it on an uneven sidewalk. The injury seems to have only gotten worse with time, as a letter from her written almost two years later expressed her concern for the upkeep of her home "if I never should walk again."[289] The injury seems to have made it difficult for her to stand for long periods of time, thus limiting her presence at formal occasions and gatherings in the White House. Finally, in a dark reenactment of the death of President William Henry Harrison, Abigail Fillmore developed pneumonia, which some contemporaries blamed on her attending Franklin Pierce's inauguration in 1853. She lingered on in agony for three weeks, and despite cupping and the use of poultices, died on March 30, 1853.

A similar situation unfolded with Eliza McCardle Johnson, the wife of President Andrew Johnson. At some point in the 1850s, Eliza contracted tuberculosis, a disease that would slowly take her life over the next twenty years. Her periodic coughing fits kept her behind Confederate lines in Tennessee while her husband was with Union forces in Nashville. When ordered along with other pro-Union sympathizers to leave the state, Eliza Johnson boldly informed the local Confederate commander that her condition would not allow for it. When her husband became president after the death of Lincoln in 1865, it took her almost four months to join him in Washington. Once in the White House, she largely stayed confined to her room. Eliza Johnson would outlive her husband, however, dying several months after he did in 1875.

Tuberculosis also took the life of Benjamin Harrison's wife, Caroline Scott, during his reelection campaign in 1892. Her death brought a halt to the campaigns of both parties and limited Harrison's ability to counter Grover Cleveland's momentum, which led to his subsequent loss. Four years later he remarried, taking the thirty-seven-year-old niece of his deceased wife as his new bride. The marriage caused a minor scandal within the nation and a feud within his family much like that of the Tylers a half-century before.

Though the medical history of President William McKinley has already been recounted in some detail, the various issues confronting his wife were no less interesting. Ida Saxton had married William McKinley in 1871, and the two seem to have enjoyed a happy marriage. Little documentation exists concerning her early health, but she appears to have complained of headaches, the causes of which can only be speculated about. These minor occurrences turned serious in the mid-1870s following the tragic death of her two children. Ida McKinley seems to have suffered from seizures, headaches, digestive issues, and debilitating menstrual cycles. Most literature describes her illness as epilepsy, brought on by the emotional strains she was under. As the condition was not well-understood at the time, treatment largely consisted of isolating the patient and administering laudanum or bromides. Ida would be heavily sedated with these drugs throughout her time in the White House.[290]

Her time in the White House was largely spent in isolation, crocheting slippers for visitors and auctions for charities. When she did appear at public events she usually remained seated with flowers in her lap. This was due not only to her epilepsy but phlebitis as well. Her first serious attack following her husband's victory in 1896 occurred at his inauguration ball in March 1897. Upon seeing the first lady, a visitor at the time stated that "her color was ghastly."[291] McKinley went to great lengths to care for his wife. In fact, in violation of tradition and protocol, Ida was kept at her husband's side during dinners. Should she suffer a seizure, the president would nonchalantly place a napkin over her face to cover her contorted features. If the attack were serious, he would excuse himself and wheel the first lady from the room. It appears that McKinley would often interrupt his work to check on his beloved wife. In fact in April 1898, at the height of deliberations over war with Spain, the president was preoccupied with his wife's health. He confided to a friend that due to her health he was sleeping no more than two or three hours a night.[292] Ida McKinley only worsened as time went on and was finally destroyed by her husband's assassination in 1901. Though she apparently did not experience another seizure, she died in isolation in 1907.

Another first lady to be plagued by ill health and paralysis was Helen Taft. After watching her morbidly obese husband undergo a series of operations, and the suffering of her children during a variety of illnesses, her health finally broke. In May 1909, Mrs. Taft suffered a debilitating stroke while onboard the presidential yacht, the USS *Mayflower*. The right side of her body became paralyzed and she lost the ability to speak. Her husband kept her condition from the public for as long as possible and spent months teaching her how to speak again. Except for hosting the couple's star-studded silver anniversary celebration on the White House lawn, Helen Taft largely removed herself from official duties for the rest of her husband's time in office. She eventually recovered, and led a renowned life until her death in 1943. Her substantial influence on her husband is well-known, yet some have argued that her stroke prevented her from successfully advising William H. Taft and preventing the split in the Republican Party that helped bring Wilson to power.[293]

Overall the health of the first ladies impacted their roles and the perception of their husbands in a way comparable to the illnesses that affected the presidents. Betty Ford's battle with alcohol and Nancy Reagan's bout with breast cancer helped to catapult those issues to a national level in the 1970s and 1980s respectively, garnering the illnesses both attention and needed fund raising.

Chapter 12

FIRST FAMILY MALADIES

"There's no tragedy in life like the death of a child. Things
never get back to the way they were."
(Dwight D. Eisenhower)

The health of the children and relatives of the various presidents has not been a heavily studied subject. Yet often times the sickness or death of a child or close loved one can impact a person as much as his or her own illnesses. Family experiences with pestilence or tragedy well before their arrival at the White House have also shaped thought and policy. With so many occupants, almost all of whom had children, one does not need to look far to find numerous anecdotes of disease and sickness affecting the first families.

The Washingtons

Due most likely to his earlier medical history, George Washington never fathered any children with Martha. He did become very attached to his stepchildren and followed their health and setbacks personally. Martha Dandridge had first been married to Daniel Parke Custis, a wealthy plantation owner. The couple had four children, two of whom would die in childhood and one of whom would die at the age of seventeen from an epileptic seizure. Martha's fourth child, John Parke Custis, was described as something of an indifferent student who married at a very young age, much to the consternation of George and Martha. Though Washington managed to convince his stepson to attend King's University in New York City in 1773, John left a year later following the death of his younger sister.

Instead of returning to school, John Parke Custis followed his step-father on his various campaigns of the war. It was in this role that he accompanied Washington to his greatest victory at Yorktown. At some point during the siege he contracted typhus, and after declining rapidly he died from the disease on November 5, 1781, only three weeks after the surrender of Cornwallis. Custis left behind a young widow and several children, most of whom were subsequently raised by the Washingtons at Mount Vernon. More important to posterity was Custis's association with a young British officer while stationed at Boston. Sometime before the latter evacuated, he gave a small plant to Custis, who planted it at his home at Abingdon. This was actually the first introduction of the willow tree to America, a plant that would flourish and find its way across the nation.[294]

The Adamses

The Adams family continued the tradition of American political clans who reached both the heights of civic accomplishments and the doldrums of personal tragedy. John and Abigail had six children over the course of their marriage, three girls and three boys. Two of the children died young, including Grace Susanna, who perished at the age of thirteen months after being born quite sickly, and Abigail's last child, Elizabeth, who was stillborn in 1777. After these initial misfortunes, most of the Adams' remaining children experienced tragic deaths as well.

The family's eldest daughter, Abigail, was born in 1765, and grew up in the shadow of the Revolution, her life becoming intertwined with the great struggles and accomplishments of her parents. By the time of the early republic, young Abigail had emerged as something of a contemporary figure. She eventually married William Stephens Smith, a man who would go on to become a United States representative and an active revolutionary in South America. In February 1811, Abigail wrote to her parents about a lump that had developed on one of her breasts. While John and Abigail wisely asked her to come to Boston at once to seek medical help, she delayed her arrival until June.

By the time she entered the city, her cancer was already quite advanced. The various doctors that Abigail Adams Smith consulted assured her of a speedy recovery and prescribed hemlock pills to aid in shrinking the tumor. Despite these rosy prognostications, Dr. Benjamin Rush soon wrote to Abigail:

> After the experience of more than 50 years in cases similar to hers, I must protest against all local applications and internal medicines for relief. They now and then cure, but in 19 cases out of 20 in tumors in the breast they do harm or suspend the disease until it passes beyond that time in which the only radical remedy is ineffectual. This remedy is the knife. From her account of the moving state of the tumor, it is now in a proper situation for the operation. Should she wait till it suppurates or even inflames much, it may be too late... I repeat again, let there be no delay in flying to the knife. Her time of life calls for expedition in this business... I sincerely sympathize with her and with you and your dear Mrs. Adams in this family affliction, but it will be but for a few minutes if she submits to have it extirpated, and if not, it will probably be a source of distress and pain to you all for years to come. It shocks me to think of the consequences of procrastination.[295]

The Adams agreed to follow Rush's advice and sought out John and Joseph Warren to perform a mastectomy. The operation took place on October 8, 1811, and lasted for about 25 minutes. During this time Abigail was tied to a chair with Dr. Warren straddling her legs. Her entire breast was cut off and many of her lymph nodes removed. Given the absence of anesthesia, Adams must have been in considerable pain, but her countenance bore up nicely as she never cried out once during the surgery or the cauterizing of her wound.

Rush and the Adams seemed relieved and confident following the operation and the fact that Abigail did not succumb to a bacterial infection was both promising and shocking, considering the complete lack of cleanliness during the surgery. But the primitive method of the procedure failed to remove all of the cancerous cells from her body. Within weeks she began to complain of both abdominal pains and headaches, which were simply written off by her doctors as rheumatism. By the spring of 1813, it was finally admitted that her cancer had spread and was by this point beyond control. Slowly wasting away, "a monument to Suffering and to Patience," Abigail Adams Smith died on August 9, 1813, leaving behind her husband and four children.[296] Thomas Jefferson took the opportunity to comfort her father, his formerly estranged friend, writing "I am silent. I know the depth of the affliction it has caused, and can sympathize with it the more sensibly, inasmuch as there is no degree of affliction produced by the loss of those dear to us, while experience has not taught me to estimate. I have found time and silence are the only medicine, and these but assuage, they never can suppress, the deep drawn sigh which recollection for ever brings up, until recollection and life are extinguished together."[297]

The fourth child of the family, Charles Adams, was yet another tragic figure. From an early age he seems to have become addicted to alcohol, becoming what his mother termed "no man's enemy but his own."[298] Charles was involved in a drunken streaking incident at Harvard, and after graduating, fell in with Baron Friedrich von Steuben and several other notorious characters in New York City. Despite marrying, he never fully settled down, consistently facing money issues and turning more towards alcohol. By late 1800, he had abandoned both his career and family, and his mother wrote that ". . . his constitution was so shaken, the disease was rapid."[299] On November 30, 1800, only three weeks after losing re-election to Thomas Jefferson, John Adams lost his second son as well, to cirrhosis of the liver.

A similar fate affected John and Abigail's youngest son, Thomas Boylston Adams, who was born in 1772 and died in 1832. Famously described by his nephew as "a brute in manners and a bully in his family," he seems to have failed at a number of endeavors and slowly descended into alcoholism. Various other illnesses also afflicted him and further served to handicap both his professional and personal life, and he died in 1832.

The Jeffersons

As was mentioned above, the birth of six children further damaged Martha Wayles Jefferson's already frail constitution and helped to hasten her early death in September 1782. Of the children themselves, four died very early in life, the majority within a year of being born. Lucy

Jefferson, who was born in 1782, shortly before Martha's death, lived for two years before falling "a Martyr to the Complicated evils of teething, Worms and Hooping Cough which last was carried there by the Virus of their friends without their knowing it was in their train."[300] Gathering from Thomas Jefferson's surviving correspondence, he and his wife seem to have been predictably distraught over the death of their children.

Of their two children who survived to adulthood, Mary (Maria) Jefferson, who was born in 1778, most resembled her mother in both beauty and frailty of health. She was "singularly beautiful. She was high-principled, just, and generous. Her temper, naturally mild, became, I think, saddened by ill health in the latter part of her life. In that respect she differed from my mother, whose disposition seemed to have the sunshine of heaven in it."[301] Much like her mother she experienced much difficulty in childbirth, and two out of her three children died shortly after being born. When her last child, a girl, died in March 1804, only a month after birth, Maria's spirit finally broke. She died a month later, most likely of complications from childbirth.

The death of Jefferson's youngest surviving daughter at least served a partially beneficial purpose. Abigail Adams, who had been a friend to her, and who had only just recently lost her own son, took the opportunity to write to the formerly close friend of her husband:

The attachment which I formed for her, when you committed her to my care: upon her arrival in a foreign Land: has remained with me to this hour...It has been some time since that I conceived of any event in this Life, which could call forth, feelings of mutual sympathy. But I know how closely entwined around a parents heart, are these chords which bind the filial to the parental Bosom, and when snaped asunder, how agonizing the pangs of seperation. I have tasted the bitter cup, and bow with reverence, and humility before the greater dispenser of it, without whose permission, and over ruling providence, not a sparrow falls to the ground. That you may derive comfort and consolation in this day of your sorrow and affliction, from that only source calculated to heal the wounded heart—a firm belief in the Being: perfections and attributes of God, is the sincere and ardent wish of her, who once took pleasure in subscribing Herself your Friend.[302]

Jefferson thanked her for her concern, and seemed to offer a hope of thawing the relationship between him and Adams:

I…am thankful for the occasion furnished me of expressing my regret that the circumstances should have arisen which have seemed to draw a line of separation between us. […] Mr. Adams's friendship and mine began at an earlier date. It accompanied us thro' long and important scenes. The different conclusions we had drawn from our political reading and reflections were not permitted to lessen mutual esteem, each party being conscious they were the result of an honest conviction in the other. Like differences of opinion existing among our fellow citizens attached them to the one or the other of us, and produced a rivalship in their minds which did not exist in ours. […] I can say with truth that one act of Mr. Adams's life, and one only, ever gave me a moment's personal displeasure. I did consider his last appointments to office as personally unkind. They were from among my most ardent political enemies, from whom no faithful cooperation could ever be expected, and laid me under the embarrasment of acting thro' men whose views were to defeat mine; or to encounter the odium of putting others in their places. […] If my respect for him did not permit me to ascribe the whole blame to the influence of others, it left something for friendship to forgive, and after brooding over it for some little time, and not always resisting the expression of it, I forgave it cordially, and returned to the same state of esteem and respect for him which had so long subsisted. […] That you may both be favored with health, tranquility and long life, is the prayer of one who tenders you the assurances of his highest consideration and esteem.[303]

These letters would initiate the process that would see the two men once again exchanging letters, producing over two decades of documents that are philosophically, politically, and historically invaluable to the nation.

John Quincy Adams

John Adams and his son John Quincy shared more than just their brilliant minds and possession of the White House. Both families were visited with unspeakable tragedy as well. As previously mentioned, the relationship between John Quincy Adams and his wife, Louisa Catherine Johnson, was severely strained by the death of their young daughter while they were in Russia. Worse was to come, however, as two of their remaining three sons would meet tragic deaths similar to those of John Quincy's brothers.

George Washington Adams, who was born in 1801, grew up in the shadow of his successful father and grandfather. Like them, he graduated from Harvard, briefly practiced law, and then entered the field of politics, doing so in 1826. Yet he seems to have fallen victim to the Adams family curse of womanizing, alcoholism, and depression, in part due to his own weaknesses of character and in part due to the legendary harsh and distant parenting of his father. His life began to spiral downward only a few months after his father exited the White House, until on June 9, 1829, he jumped or fell from the steamship *Benjamin Franklin* while it was sailing through Long Island Sound. His body washed ashore some six weeks later and was buried by his heartbroken father in the family crypt. George's suicide also brought to light a bastard child that had been born with a local maid, a situation that led to the blackmail of the Adams family.

Further tragedy followed five years later when John Adams II died from a combination of alcoholism and stress. While Charles Francis Adams would go on to achieve great renown, much as John Quincy had done, it seemed for both generations that greatness and vitality had to be siphoned off from other siblings, leaving the achievement almost bittersweet.

James K. Polk

Presidents have been varied in terms of politics, experience, success, height, religion, and even their number of children. Though one of our more neglected and underrated presidents, John Tyler was undoubtedly the most prolific leader of the nation in terms of offspring. Over the course of forty-five years, his two wives bore him fifteen children. In addition, there were frequent attacks on him alleging that he also had fathered numerous children with his female slaves. As has been seen with George Washington, Andrew Jackson, and others, not all presidents had children. While some may have done so out of choice, for others, like George Washington, it was the result of disease related sterility. For James K. Polk, it was a much more tragic occurrence.

Polk, who was born in 1795, appears to have suffered from several health issues during his childhood. Perhaps the worst of these was an attack of bladder stones, followed by a hernia which left him practically immobilized. The sixteen-year-old Polk was brought all the way to Dr. Ephraim McDowell, a famed frontier surgeon who only six years before had performed the world's first recorded, successful ovariotomy (surgical incision of an ovary). The 250-mile trip on horseback must have been excruciatingly painful for the young man, but he eventually arrived at the doctor's home on Second Street in Danville, Kentucky. From all accounts, the surgery appears to have been a success, but with Polk's subsequent inability to have children, were there unforeseen side effects?

The operation has been credited with having altered Polk's previously lackadaisical life, since a noted change occurred in the young man following the removal of the urinary stone and the hernia repair. Polk himself, in a letter he is alleged to have written to Dr. McDowell several years later stated:

> I have been enabled to obtain an education, study the profession of law, and embark successfully in the practice; have married a wife, and permanently settled in Tennessee; and now occupy the station in which the good wishes of my fellow-citizens have placed me. When I reflect, the contrast is great, indeed, between the boy, the meagre boy with pallid cheeks, oppressed and worn down with disease, when he first presented himself to your kind notice, in Danville, nearly 14 years ago, and the man at this day in the full enjoyment of health.[304]

The relief the young Polk experienced reinvigorated him, and though now sterile, his rise to power and his subsequent accomplishments while in office led to a dramatic sea change in American foreign policy. The western lands between the Louisiana Purchase and the Pacific Ocean were now firmly American, trade was opened with Asia, and the slow progression towards the Civil War began to pick up steam.

Zachary Taylor

Zachary Taylor's death while in office has already been shown to have helped prevent the outbreak of civil war. Unwittingly, the famous general bore another connection to the Civil War after it finally did break out. Out of Taylor's five daughters, two died in 1820, both under the age of four, from "bilious fever." After his eldest daughter married a career soldier and moved off to the distant frontier, General Taylor became much more concerned with his remaining two children's futures.

In the early 1830s, when his second daughter, Sarah Knox Taylor, was courted by Lt. Jefferson Davis, Taylor was opposed to the match. To placate his new father-in-law, Davis resigned his commission in the army and settled down on a plantation in Mississippi. The couple was duly married on June 17, 1835, and traveled to Louisiana that summer. Unfortunately their visit was at the height of the malaria season and both were stricken with the disease. Shortly thereafter, on September 15, Sarah died. Taylor blamed Davis for Sarah's death, and Davis spent years in seclusion before once again entering politics. In the end, though Taylor's actions would help delay the impending Civil War, although his former son-in-law would eventually help bring it to fruition, becoming the first president of the Confederacy.

Millard Fillmore

As they do with several other nineteenth-century presidents, the American public largely forgets Millard Fillmore. Students are taught simply that his presidency followed that of Zachary Taylor, and that the largest accomplishments of his term were the Compromise of 1850 and the fact that he dispatched Commodore Matthew Perry to Japan, thereby opening that country to the West. More interesting perhaps was Fillmore's attempt to run for the presidency in 1856, four years after having left national office.

By this time the Whig Party had dissolved, largely due to its inability to address the issue of slavery and the national anger expressed at the passing of the Kansas-Nebraska Act. Rather than join the rising Republican Party, Fillmore was nominated as the standard bearer of the American Party. In the end he secured almost 22 percent of the national vote and carried the state of Maryland. Yet what stands out in this entire episode was the platform of the American Party itself. More widely known as the Know-Nothings, the party was virulently anti-immigration, anti-alcohol, and anti-Catholic. Many biographers have stressed that Fillmore himself was far from bigoted against Catholics, supporting this view by pointing out that he enrolled his daughter in a local Catholic school and had himself donated money towards the construction of St. Joseph's Cathedral in Buffalo, New York.

However, his actions can easily be explained away. His donations to the church were more likely of a purely political nature than a statement of respect for the religion, coming as they did at the height of his campaign efforts. Historically Fillmore is said to have re-entered politics only following the death of his beloved daughter. His wife, Abigail Powers, had also died only a year before, succumbing to pneumonia several weeks after Fillmore left office. Loneliness has been argued to be the main force driving him back into the political arena, but disease could have played a role as well.

On July 26, 1854, Fillmore's only daughter, Mary Abigail, died of cholera. While the death may have pushed the former president back into the political mileau, the nature of it may have been what drove him into the American Party. Arriving as it did aboard the Irish coffin ships and striking mostly the poor, cholera was seen as a disease of dirt and poverty in the miasmic view of the day. James Fenimore Cooper reported, ". . . cholera is in America, but I should not think it will prove a very bad disease among a people so well fed and so clean."[305] Since pestilence does not distinguish between class or race, the illness soon struck all Americans, leading to anger, recrimination, and even deadly violence against the Irish. Many states and localities enacted harsh laws to turn back the perceived hordes of diseased immigrants descending upon America, and it was in this atmosphere that the Know-Nothings arose. Fillmore's adherence to a party whose platform detailed its opposition to both Catholics as well as foreigners was not by accident or by lack of political choices, but due to his daughter dying from an Irish Catholic disease.

Franklin Pierce

Joining the likes of John Tyler and Millard Fillmore was Franklin Pierce, a man solely remembered for his lackluster performance during the slow creep towards the calamity of the Civil War. Yet the tragedies visited upon Pierce's small family may have played a role in his failure to assert himself once in office. With almost a decade of service in Congress and a brief, illness-filled stint in the army during the Mexican War, Pierce had built up a resume similar to other men seeking higher office, but his family appears to have suffered in his absences. His first son, Franklin Jr., died in 1836, only a few days after his birth. As Jane Pierce wrote to her sister, "I have been thinking of my precious child much today...he was in my dreams last night...it is desolate to be without him."[306] Likewise the couple's second child, Frank Robert, died from typhus at the age of four. Still, the small Pierce family carried on until the election of Franklin to the presidency in 1852.

After winning the election, Pierce, his wife, and his sole surviving son, Benjamin, departed on a private railcar from Boston to Lawrence, Massachusetts. On January 6, 1853, the train broke an axle, throwing Pierce's car over an embankment and down a slope. Though many were injured in the accident, the only casualty was the president-elect's eleven-year-year old son Benjamin. After being crushed to death in front of his father and perennially ailing mother, Benny's demise would weigh heavily on his parents. The first lady took to writing letters to her dead children and refrained from taking an active role within the White House. At the same time, President Pierce became more and more dominated by pro-slavery Southerners in his party. By the time he left office in 1857 his parting remarks were, "All that's left, is to drink and die," a promise he would fulfill a decade later.

Abraham Lincoln

Perhaps no family suffered more tragedy while residing in the White House than the Lincolns, since the majority of the family suffered either untimely deaths or bouts of mental illness. The first such calamity occurred in 1850 when the Lincoln's second son, Edward Baker, died just short of his fourth birthday. Traditionally his cause of death has been given as consumption, an earlier term for tuberculosis, yet more recent research has proposed additional causes. Dr. John Sotos has suggested that Lincoln and his son both suffered from multiple endocrine neoplasia type 2B, or MEN2B. Genetically inherited, the disease could have very easily killed young Eddie and perhaps his father as well, had he lived several more years.[307]

The worst was yet to come after the Lincolns entered the White House. The masses of Union soldiers camped around the capital helped to spread an epidemic of typhoid, which ravaged Washington in 1862. Both eleven-year-old Willie and eight-year-old Tad contracted the illness and suffered for weeks. On February 20, Willie died, sending Mary Todd Lincoln deep into fits of depression. The first lady's sanity had been suspect for years. Now during her time of inconsolable grief, Lincoln famously approached her, saying, "Mother, do you see that large white building on the hill yonder? Try and control your grief, or it will drive you mad, and we may have to send you there." The president's threats to have her confined to the nearby sanatorium did little to help her condition. Likewise, a carriage accident the next year on July 2, 1863, which caused her a slight head injury, became magnified in Mary's mind to be an assassination attempt against the president.

The final tragedy for the family came in July 1871. Thomas "Tad" Lincoln had been born in 1853 with a cleft palette that severely limited his ability to speak and be understood. His upbringing was tarnished by the Civil War, the various deaths in his family, and the loose parenting style of his father. Following the assassination of the president, Tad and his brother lived for a while in Chicago, where the former attended school. Suddenly on July 15, 1871, Thomas Lincoln died, delivering one last tragedy to the family. The causes of his demise have been debated ever since, with some sources arguing for tuberculosis or pneumonia, while others suggesting congestive heart failure. Contemporary newspapers simply referred to it vaguely as "dropsy of the chest."[308]

Benjamin Harrison

The untimely death of William Henry Harrison was not the only tragedy to befall that great military and political family. The former president's son, John Scott Harrison, fathered thirteen children of his own, five of whom died in infancy. Much like his father, he studied medicine and also abandoned the subject to pursue other fields. After a disease-filled and challenging life, John Scott Harrison died on May 25, 1878. As grave robbing was a commonplace evil at the time, his son Benjamin Harrison concocted a series of elaborate ruses and precautions to protect his deceased father's body. Even with these actions, John Scott Harrison's body was stolen and was discovered by accident a day later hanging in a secret room at the Ohio Medical College. His own son, Carter Harrison, found him while searching for the missing body of another friend. It seems that the men hired to guard the grave had instead made off with the body.[309]

It is not surprising that presidents and their families sought to limit the impacts of disease whenever possible, but Benjamin Harrison had a personal reason for doing so. Harrison was inaugurated as president on March 4, 1889, exactly forty-eight years to the day since his grandfather had become the ninth president. His ancestor's fate following his lengthy inaugural address was as well-known to the new president as it was to the general public. To protect himself during his own cold and rainy swearing in, Benjamin Harrison not only gave a very brief speech but also wore a full frock coat heavily lined with chamois, and used an umbrella. Though his precautions paid off in the short term, he ironically died twelve years later from pneumonia, the same illness that killed his grandfather. Continued concern over the potential health risk of a March inauguration prompted a Congressional proposal on May 10, 1898, to move date of the inauguration to the last Thursday in April.

Many other presidents lost children as well, and though not every child and every disease can be shown to have specifically altered a presidency, the emotional impact would certainly have changed the sum total of the man. William McKinley lost both of his children to disease, which only further upset his wife's mental condition. The death in combat of Teddy Roosevelt's son Quentin helped to break the once indomitable man and hasten his death. Roosevelt summed his feelings up by saying, "I shall never cease bitterly regretting that I was not allowed to go to the other side. I would not have expected to come home alive. But at times it seems almost more than I can bear to have my sons face dreadful danger while I sit at home in ease and comfort and safety. It is a terrible thing that death should come to the young."[310] This was not a purely eighteenth- and nineteenth-century problem.

Both the Kennedys and the Bushes lost a young child, which greatly affected the psyches of both the parents and the surviving children. John and Jackie's first child, Arabella, as well as their last, Patrick, died at birth. Speculation exists that Jack's chlamydia could have helped complicate his wife's pregnancies, further alienating the two. George H.W. and Barbara Bush's elder daughter, Robin, died of leukemia just short of her fourth birthday. The death profoundly affected both Bushes and was brought up as a topic during debates decades later. George W. Bush's belief in "compassionate conservatism" arose in part due to this tragedy that he faced during his formative years.[311] In 2015, the death of Vice President Joseph Biden's son was claimed as one of the prime motivating factors keeping him from entering the race for president. Though once again this may have simply been political cover to watch from the sidelines, it was plausible to many sympathetic Americans.

Regardless of the time period, the death of a child profoundly affected all presidents as it would anyone else. Depression, apathy while in office, a move towards compassion, or even a push to leave one's political mark on the world now that a biological one has been erased—all resulted from these deaths. In essence, these tragedies affected the psychological health of the men in the Oval Office in a way similar to that of the viruses and bacteria.

The Cabinet

While clearly the health of the president has been paramount in our study of disease and government, several notable events have shown that the illnesses that affected those around him could have an equally profound influence on American history. Washington formed the first cabinet out of perceived necessity shortly after his inauguration rather than because of an actual constitutional requirement. Since that time, the brilliance of his decision has been shown by the continued growth of the number of departments within the federal government. A thorough analysis of these men and women reveals the familiar specter of ill health that troubled so many presidents.

Fifteen cabinet members have died while in office, a number that mirrors the presidents and vice presidents who also passed away while in government service. The difference perhaps lies in the fact that many of these men and women were not household names and that most of their accomplishments became elided into the legacies of their respective presidencies. In addition not every illness or death is important in and of itself, thus supporting the fading away of the memory of many of these secretaries. Yet amidst the trivia of many of these illnesses several important milestone episodes emerge.

This is especially true concerning the health of the secretary of state. Often considered the first among equals, the position has elevated many men to the presidency and has often driven the policy of the country more than the man in the White House. Overall, seven men who headed the State Department either died in office or had to step down due to illness. The first to do so was Abel Upshur who perished in 1844 along with the secretary of the navy and four other individuals as a result of the USS *Princeton* disaster. While Upshur's death did not drastically alter American foreign policy, the deaths or resignations of James G. Blaine in 1881 and 1892, John Sherman in 1898, John Hay in 1905, Cordell Hull in 1944, and John Foster Dulles in 1959 did strip away very talented and well-respected professional diplomats.

Perhaps the greatest change followed the death in office of the little-known Walter Quintin Gresham. Originally a Republican from Indiana, Gresham had ridden into Congress on the Republican wave of 1860 that precipitated the Civil War. Not content with simply legislating victory, the young Hoosier volunteered as an officer in the United States Army and participated in numerous battles and campaigns, including the fight for Vicksburg and the Battle of Atlanta. After being wounded during Sherman's March to the Sea, he was forced out of the military and returned to politics. Though he served as postmaster general and the secretary of the treasury in Chester Arthur's administration, and attempted to run for the presidency in 1884 and 1888, he became a Mugwump in 1892 and supported Grover Cleveland for president.

Once elected for his second term in the White House, Cleveland rewarded Gresham by appointing him secretary of state. His rise to power came at a time when many citizens were beginning to flirt with the idea of America assuming a larger role in world affairs. Cleveland was specifically confronted with a border dispute between Venezuela and the United Kingdom, a growing rebellion in Cuba, and a pro-American annexation movement in Hawaii. Gresham worked to better relations with the world and sought to disentangle the nation from many foreign affairs. Most notably he fought to convince Cleveland to abandon America's position in Samoa and sought to diffuse tensions with Japan and Germany, and between various Central American states. Non-interventionism was dealt a blow when Secretary Gresham unexpectedly died.

Apparently Gresham had been in ill health for some time, having suffered from stomach problems, and once even having been bedridden for a full year. His final illness seems to have struck in early May and was assumed at the time to be an attack of gallstones. It wasn't until almost two days later that doctors diagnosed the true cause as pleurisy. His left lung quickly filled with fluid, which his already weakened condition prevented his doctors from draining. Despite the administration of strychnine and other stimulants, Gresham died on May 28, 1895.[312]

Richard Olney, the attorney general, replaced Gresham. Olney proved to be much more of an internationalist than Gresham, and his efforts increased the prestige and presence of the United States abroad. Perhaps Olney's greatest accomplishment was his involvement in the border dispute between the United Kingdom and Venezuela. While Gresham and Cleveland had largely followed the letter of the Monroe Doctrine, seeing this as a legitimate dispute between a European and American nation, Olney took a more evolved approach. Writing to Lord Salisbury, the American secretary of state defined the "Olney Doctrine," which described the nation's special interest in all conflicts in the Western Hemisphere: "Today the United States is practically sovereign on this continent and its fiat is law upon the subjects to which it confines its interposition. Why? It is because, in addition to all other grounds, its infinite resources combined with its isolated position render it master of the situation and practically invulnerable as against any or all other powers."[313] Olney's alteration of American foreign policy would begin the nation's lurch towards imperialism that would crystallize under Cleveland's immediate successors. The Olney Doctrine itself would quickly transform into the Roosevelt Corollary of the Monroe Doctrine and guarantee a century of American involvement in the Caribbean and Latin America.

Modern medicine has not exempted cabinet officials from health concerns any more than it has done so to presidents. As recently as 2004, Attorney General John Ashcroft was hospitalized with acute gallstone pancreatitis. While such a diagnosis and associated operation would not normally cause national concern, accompanying current events elevated Ashcroft's condition immensely. Just before his hospitalization, the Justice Department had ruled that President George W. Bush's NSA-run domestic surveillance program was illegal. Though Ashcroft had empowered James Comey, his deputy, to handle the department's affairs in his absence, the president sent his chief of staff and the White House counsel to the hospital to convince Ashcroft to overrule the department's decision, since Comey refused to do so. In response, Comey and FBI director Robert Mueller likewise raced to George Washington University Hospital to back up the ailing attorney general. A dramatic bedside debate took place after which Ashcroft refused to sign the papers and both Comey and Mueller threatened to resign should they be overruled. The Bush administration eventually backed down, agreeing to change certain elements of the program with which the Justice Department disagreed.

The health of those surrounding the president can be as important as that of the chief executive himself. The sickness of children can have a psychological impact, as seen with Polk, Lincoln, and Bush, or can serve to shape a series of choices in life. At the same time, presidents who follow a more managerial leadership style tend to lean heavily on their cabinet. Therefore, any health issues or deaths within that group of advisors can alter policy and change the direction of both the president and the nation. Concern for the health of those who were immediately around them has also pushed many presidents to begin to consider the health of the nation as a whole to be within their personal and political bailiwick.

Chapter 13

THE FIRST CITIZEN

"We should resolve now that the health of this nation is a
national concern."
(Harry S. Truman, 1945)

Philosophers such as Aristotle, St. Augustine, Machiavelli, and Confucius, men from both East and West, have discussed for years the connection between the virtue of a civilization and its vitality. In keeping with this line of thinking, it is not farfetched to likewise find a causal relationship between the health of citizens and the well-being of their nation. Early experiences with the impact of disease upon the settlement of the colonies and the victory over the British in 1783 had driven both individuals and communities towards such formerly controversial ideas as inoculation and public sanitation. With the growth of the country and the personal experiences of both presidents and congressmen with contagion, it was inevitable that the government began to focus more upon improving the health of the overall nation. Numerous officials took a personal interest in this topic, no doubt due in part to their own past health concerns. This was not a static campaign however, for as the nation grew, spread, and advanced so, too, did the threat from contagion. The growth of disease both paralleled and overlapped the development of advanced society. The presence of disease necessitates the development of ways to deal with it. Government, communication, science, and law all arise or advance, in part, to deal with pestilence. Advancement produces disease; disease produces advancement.

The early American colonists were restricted from successfully addressing disease in their society for scientific and religious reasons. The settlers at Jamestown invited their "Starving Time" by settling in a malarial swamp and drinking contaminated, brackish water. In fact the term itself is something of a misnomer. What almost doomed Jamestown and Virginia was not a lack of food, but disease. Over its first winter a hundred colonists would indeed starve, but thousands would die over the next decade from a variety of both native and foreign pathogens. Only the chance digging of a clean well by a group of segregated Poles helped to prevent the complete destruction of the settlement. A generation later, the Pilgrims at Plymouth lost most of their initial settlers to scurvy, tuberculosis, and pneumonia. Though both of these settlements recovered, disease continued to appear periodically, challenging both government and church.

A Calvinist view of disease largely kept the inhabitants of Boston from accepting variolation when the process emerged around 1700. Cotton Mather, who had lost two wives and nine children to illness, became a surprising supporter of the procedure during the smallpox epidemic of 1721. During the summer of that year more than 10 percent of the city had fled and 1 percent had died during the outbreak. Mather began to write about and preach the saving power of variolation: "The grievous Calamity of the Small-Pox has now entered the Town. The Practice of conveying and suffering the Small-pox by Inoculation, has never been used in America, nor indeed in our Nation. But how many Lives might be saved by it, if it were prasticed?"[314] Mather and Dr. Zabdiel Bolyston began to inoculate hundreds of people, and received verbal assaults and a grenade attack by a religious zealot in response to their efforts:

> At this Time, I enjoy and unspeakable Consolation. I have instructed our Physicians in the new Method used by the Africans and Asiaticks, to prevent and abate the Dangers of the Small-Pox.... The Destroyer, being enraged at the Proposal of any Thing, that may rescue the Lives of our poor People from him, has taken a strange Possession of the People on this Occasion. They rave, they rail, they blaspheme; they talk not only like Ideots but also like Franticks, And not only the Physician who began the Experiment, but I also am an Object of their Fury.[315]

The federal government's first attempts to affect public health can be traced to the time of the Revolution. As discussed previously, Washington's personal beliefs as well as strategic thought led to the mass inoculation of the American army at Valley Forge. Shortly after the start of the republic, Congress passed "An Act for the Relief of Sick and Disabled Seamen," which mandated that sailors were required to pay twenty cents per month to help construct marine hospitals for sick sailors. Though an esoteric law, this piece of legislation reemerged in the public sphere during the debate over the constitutionality of the Affordable Care Act 220 years later.[316] Yet for the immediate future most of the efforts undertaken to combat disease or improve health were state-run enterprises.

The majority of the government's efforts at public health remained confined to the military. In the 1820s and 1830s Surgeon General of the Army Joseph Lovell sought, to improve the sanitation of army camps, adopted new regulations and mandated periodic reports. He also purchased heavier winter clothing for the soldiers and set up the Weather Bureau, which eventually evolved into the National Weather Service. The government went so far as to mandate smallpox vaccines for all incoming soldiers. Around the same time, Congress passed the Vaccine Act of 1813, which nationalized the production, storage, and distribution of smallpox vaccines. Continued epidemics and the advent of interstate travel led to the passage of the National Quarantine Act of 1878 as well, increasing the oversight power of the federal government.

The majority of public health undertakings were done on the state level in the nineteenth century, in keeping with the political thought of the era. This would change with the advent of Progressivism and the presidency of Teddy Roosevelt. In the minds of many, the interrelated elements of industrialization, urbanization, and immigration necessitated increased government intervention. One of the earliest forms of this involvement concerned federal efforts to ban alcohol, which eventually coalesced into the Eighteenth Amendment, and certain drugs, which were prohibited under the Harrison Narcotics Act of 1914. To help facilitate this, the position of surgeon general was created in 1871 for Dr. John Maynard Woodworth.

Children became the natural target for these efforts, with public education becoming a useful and practical tool in the fight against widespread disease. Besides the compulsory vaccination laws aimed at children, local schools began to incorporate health classes and programs into their curricula. One of the most famous of these was the Modern Health Crusade, a program begun by the National Tuberculosis Association in 1917. An outgrowth of the Christmas Seal program, itself popularized by famed muckraker Jacob Riis, was the Modern Health Crusade that was aimed at improving the eating and sanitary habits of poor children, who were often the hardest hit by tuberculosis.

The Modern Health Crusade centered on students completing a variety of health chores. These included examinations of posture, the consumption of milk and grains, the movement of bowels, and proper washing. The entire system was cloaked in a medieval storyline in which children endeavored to rise through the ranks of an imaginary feudal hierarchy. Romantic tales of heroes and legends from the Lancelot Grail Cycle were incorporated into the program as a way to interest the youth. Students would report their daily hygiene and eating activities in order to garner points. These would be awarded with appropriate medieval prizes and move students through a series of ranks from squire to Knight Banneret Constant. Weight was a closely associated element, as it was felt that underweight children were more susceptible to disease, an ironic concern considering America's obsession with childhood obesity today.

By 1922, over seven million children across the country were involved in the program. Interschool "tournaments" in health were held, and an elite Order of the Round Table was established for those who performed well enough in their classes. The ideas behind the system were judged to be a success and a general health curriculum was incorporated into the educational systems of most states. The government was assuming a larger role in the care of children, especially in an area that was formerly the bailiwick of parents.

President Theodore Roosevelt's Square Deal included as one of its elements consumer protection. This idea would encompass products ranging from food to medicine and everything in between. As with most federal legislation, it would be national tragedy that would lead to its creation. In 1902, thirteen children in St. Louis died in quick succession. The investigation that was launched shortly thereafter determined the cause of death to be tainted vaccines. The sera in question were diphtheria vaccines that came from a horse that had been euthanized due to tetanus. However, some of the sera bled from the horse before its death were contaminated, resulting in the wave of deaths in St. Louis. Shortly after, a batch of tainted smallpox vaccines killed nine children in Camden, New Jersey. In response to national outrage and concern, Congress passed the 1902 Biologics Control Act, granting the authority to monitor and regulate vaccines to the Public Health Services. This lesser-known piece of legislation was joined in 1906 by the much more famous Pure Food and Drug Act, which granted the federal government the power to inspect and regulate all consumables crossing over interstate lines. Food ingredients and their effects on public health, as seen in the 1916 case, *US v. Forty Barrels and Twenty Kegs of Coca-Cola*, were now a prime governmental concern. In this famous case, the commissioner of the Food and Drug Administration sued Coca Cola not over its claim to contain cocaine, but its use of caffeine. Commissioner Harvey Wiley felt that caffeine was a substance that was harmful to the health of Americans and sued in order to both expose the amount within the product and to rouse public anger against the ingredient. Though Coca Cola technically won the lawsuit, it was pushed by public pressure to include the amount of caffeine on its product. In addition, various congressmen over the next few decades introduced legislation to have the ingredient banned in products.

This power was soon followed by the passage of the Meat Inspection Act of 1906, which established a system of food regulation unheard of in modern times. The catalyst for this momentous law was author Upton Sinclair's book The Jungle. Though the socialist writer had hoped to affect laws improving the lot of recent immigrants to America, the public was struck instead by the vivid descriptions of the unsanitary slaughtering and processing of livestock. The various diseases of the animals particularly stood out in the minds of most American readers:

It seemed that they must have agencies all over the country, to hunt out old and crippled and diseased cattle to be canned. There were cattle which had been fed on "whiskey-malt," the refuse of the breweries, and had become what the men called "steerly"—which means covered with boils. It was a nasty job killing these, for when you plunged your knife into them they would burst and splash foul-smelling stuff into your face; and when a man's sleeves were smeared with blood, and his hands steeped in it, how was he ever to wipe his face, or to clear his eyes so that he could see? It was stuff such as this that made the "embalmed beef" that had killed several times as many United States soldiers as all the bullets of the Spaniards.[317]

Nor were the animals the only ones in the factory system to be afflicted: "The workers in each of them had their own peculiar diseases. And the wandering visitor might be sceptical about all the swindles, but he could not be sceptical about these, for the worker bore the evidence of them about on his own person—generally he had only to hold out his hand."[318] These included various skin conditions, skeletal deformities, rheumatism, and blood poisoning. The various diseases of both the workers and cattle as well as associated illnesses of the consumer compelled President Roosevelt and others to reform the American meat industry.

One of the more notorious actions of the federal government with regards to disease was the Tuskegee Experiments. Starting in 1932, the United States government sponsored a long-term study of the effects of syphilis. Six hundred black men, two-thirds of whom had the disease, were lured into the study with promises of free medical care for "bad blood," free meals, and free burial insurance. Originally meant to last for six months, the program would continue for forty years. Due to the fact that the subjects were ill-informed, not treated for their condition, and in some cases prevented from acquiring outside treatment, the study goes down in medical research annals as an example of science taken too far.

The Tuskegee Institute provided researchers, doctors, nurses, and medical students to aid in the study, whose subjects were mostly illiterate sharecroppers. No effective treatment was available for the disease at the start of the experiment, and it was considered a worthwhile goal to track the effects of the illness. Yet with the adoption of penicillin as a cure for syphilis during World War II, the experiment delved deeper into the realm of unethicalness. Some of the participants who enlisted for the war were told by the draft board of their disease upon receiving a medical examination, yet the doctors in the study prevented them from receiving treatment. As late as the 1960s, a time when the disease was declining in the nation, the surviving subjects were still being fed placebos. Overall, around twenty-eight individuals in the program died of syphilis or related ailments. The experiment did not come to a halt until a whistleblower leaked the story to the press in 1972. Shortly thereafter a $10 million out-of-court settlement was reached, and the United States government agreed to provide free medical care to all participants. It is still debatable what, if anything, the study accomplished, as penicillin had become available so early into the experiment. The episode has instead come to symbolize the horrors of a utilitarian mindset in the battling of disease.

A similar experiment was being undertaken during the same time period under United States governmental auspices in the country of Guatemala. From 1946 to 1948, the Public Health Service conducted a test of penicillin and other treatments on patients with various venereal diseases. Incredibly, to obtain a viable supply of test subjects, local prostitutes were hired to infect prison inmates, soldiers, and orphans with syphilis, gonorrhea, or chlamydia. In other cases, victims would be infected directly by the PHS workers. Worse yet, seven women with epilepsy had syphilis injected directly below their skulls to test its curative property. The subjects instead developed bacterial meningitis. In a continuation of these Draconian measures, one woman who was already dying of syphilis had gonorrhea injected directly into her eyeball.[319] In all, about 1,500 people were infected with VD for the study. The entire experiment ended after only two years, and the government would not accept responsibility for its actions for nearly sixty years. As Dr. John Cutler, the head of the program, said, ". . . unless the law winks occasionally, you have no progress in medicine."

Building upon some of the above-mentioned research, Franklin Roosevelt's government passed the National Venereal Disease Control Act of 1938 as part of its desire for social transformation during the New Deal. Congress earmarked more than $15 million to help educate and treat Americans with syphilis or other venereal diseases. By 1940, close to 3,000 centers had been set up all across the country. World War II revealed even more candidly the true nature of the pandemic, as 170,000 draftees tested positive for the contagion. Rapid treatment centers were soon set up, and by the 1950s the total number of reported cases was down to 6,500. It became the progressive hope that venereal diseases, especially syphilis, would become horrors of the past within the next 10 to 20 years.

An outbreak of swine flu, or H1N1, in 1976 also sparked panic across the nation. Originating at Fort Dix, New Jersey, it originated from a similar strain as the 1918 pandemic. Fear soon began to resonate across the country. The original soldier stricken with the illness died within twenty-four hours and many more quickly fell ill. President Gerald Ford called for a massive vaccination program, and was himself photographed in the Oval Office receiving the vaccine. But the deaths of three senior citizens in October, allegedly due to the vaccines themselves, set off an anti-vaccination backlash. By December, when the outbreak was officially declared over, only 22 percent of the population had been vaccinated.

Due to a combination of economic and moral factors, the government enacted a series of far-reaching health-related programs during the Cold War, including Medicare and Medicaid, passed as part of President Lyndon Johnson's Great Society endeavor. Success in the battle against disease was costly. As insurance companies had discovered previously, preventative care and healthy living were keys to reducing disease and strengthening the economy. Johnson's programs were designed to help those unable to afford care. In addition, as contagious diseases knew no socio-economic barriers, an unhealthy, illness-ridden poor segment of the population could easily infect the healthy and rich. At the same time, others feared the move as a slow descent towards socialism. Future president Ronald Reagan achieved a bit of fame in what was called Operation Coffee Cup, a series of recordings in which citizens were encouraged to contact their congressmen to oppose the move. Conservatives feared medical shortages, increased cost, less competition, higher taxes, and government overreach.

A similar program and similar debate would rage again thirty years later. Both President Bill Clinton's attempt at healthcare reform, and later "Obamacare," were both touted in part as a means to reduce health costs by focusing on preventative medicine. This process actually began under President Dwight Eisenhower in 1955, with the creation of the President's Council on Youth Fitness. Reports at the height of the Cold War suggested that young Americans were less physically fit than those of other nations. This was not only a health issue, but a national security one as well. In response, Eisenhower created a permanent body which would encourage young people to exercise and play sports. Future presidents incorporated tests and awards into the program, and most recently nutrition became a component of it.

As part of the process, some local governments have intruded into private life, going so far as to ban certain foods or actions. The idea of a sin tax has been practiced in the country for generations, producing revenue and convincing citizens to eschew certain actions or products, more often than not for moral purposes. During the post war era, moralists teamed up with scientists and health advocates to attempt to further restrict access to such illness-causing agents as tobacco and alcohol. By the 2000s, the cost for Medicaid and prospective costs of Obamacare led to further taxes and even proscriptions. The Affordable Care Act, for instance, contained in its pages an excise tax on tanning, while at the same time such cities as Philadelphia and New York tried to tax or even ban sodas and trans-fats. In 2012, first lady Michelle Obama achieved notoriety among students in 2012 thanks to her part in a government program to forcibly redesign school lunches, and she helped establish a White House garden as an example for the nation. As the government assumes more and more of a role in the treatment of disease, one can expect additional behavioral controls to be put into place.

Epidemic diseases remain the most feared health risk for the American public, despite their slim number of fatalities per year when compared to heart disease or other conditions. New diseases, including Ebola, MERS, SARS, and MRSA, have arisen over the past few decades and spread with terrifying speed and accompanying high death rates. Outbreaks in China have led to travel bans, restrictions on movement and freedom, and even forced relocation. Some governments around the world have proposed restricting the use of antibiotics by hospitals, doctors, and on farms to slow the rise of drug resistant strains of infection such as MRSA. In 2005, President George W. Bush released the "National Strategy to Safeguard Against the Danger of Pandemic Influenza," a $7.1 billion program to identify yearly influenza strains, and stockpile vaccines for the American public. It is estimated that that disease alone claims on average 36,000 lives a year and costs the economy more than $10 billion in lost productivity. In September 2013, the Department of Homeland Security announced the creation of a twenty-four-hour live web-based reporting system designed to tract the outbreak of illness around the planet. Updated hourly and drawn from 25,000 online sources, the program would provide immediate warning and enable quick response by the government of the United States to any possible microbial threat.

At the same time that access to vaccines was near universal and the elimination of diseases was considered to be a real possibility, more and more Americans became concerned about the safety of vaccines in a way unseen since the late nineteenth century. A 1982 television documentary that blamed the DPT vaccine for disabilities in children led to both a refusal to vaccinate and massive lawsuits against the drug company Lederle. By 1985, the costs of these tort cases led to increased manufacturing costs, skyrocketing prices for vaccines, and produced shortages of vaccines. In response, Congress passed the National Childhood Vaccine Injury Act in 1986 to limit the liability of drug companies.

A similar outbreak of vaccine hysteria emerged in the 1990s as various media outlets, celebrities, and some researchers began to propose a link between autism and the presence of the mercury-based preservative thiomersal in various vaccines. Robert F. Kennedy Jr. wrote a popular and persuasive, though factually inaccurate, article for *Rolling Stone*, in which he alleged the existence of a vast conspiracy on the part of drug companies and the government.[320] However, numerous studies have cast doubt upon his theory, and various publications have edited and recanted his story. The Centers for Disease Control held a conference at Simpsonwood in Norcross, Georgia, in 2000, which presented all of the data on the subject and distributed it to the general public and researchers. This did not stop approximately 4,800 families from suing in 2007, in what became known as the Autism Omnibus Trial. The Vaccine Court, after hearing the claims of specific parties and experts from both sides, ruled against the families, finding that no conclusive connection had been proven between vaccinations and the onset of autism. The controversy did not die with the case, and the idea of a connection continues to be believed by many to the present day.

The move of the government to confront disease in its own ranks more aggressively was accompanied by increased efforts to combat contagion among the general public. Not only was this seen as morally proper and of benefit to both the economy and national security, but the old idea that disease knows neither class nor rank was found to be quite true. A pestilence outside of Washington could quickly enter the city. For all of these reasons, the past 200 years of American history has seen the steady increase in the intrusion of government into personal health issues, a trend that shows no sign of ebbing.

CONCLUSION

B ehind every great president, and at the root of most important events in American history, stood disease. With the lives of everyday people being shaped by illness, why should the leaders of the nation be any different? A central tenet that has emerged from our study is the unpredictable path that these disease-driven events can take. For instance, while in some cases sickness prevented war, in others it caused it. Likewise, it was not simply the health of the president that dictated the course of American history but sometimes that of his vice president or his family as well. When this idea is extrapolated to include illnesses that affect the cabinet or Congress, the true extent to which contagion might impact policy and alter history becomes even greater.

Clearly the most meaningful conclusion to draw from this work is the sheer variety of effects that disease had upon both presidents and the country. Illnesses prevented George Washington, Andrew Jackson, and James Knox Polk from fathering children. This helped to drive them in politics and even prevented the first president from establishing a dynasty while in office. Likewise, a certain sense of having survived serious illness, or of seeking to avoid it by establishing a legacy, or the loss of children in general, pushed such men as Polk, William McKinley, Theodore Roosevelt, Franklin Roosevelt, John F. Kennedy, and George H.W. Bush to concentrate heavily on being quite active during their terms of office. While the greatest accomplishment of such men as Genghis Khan and Charlemagne may in the end be the fecundity of their loins, this was not possible for Polk and Washington; thus a greater legacy had to be established through the presidency. Others, such as Franklin Pierce, were so drained by the loss of their children that their time in office amounted to little more than mourning and failure.

Stretching from the Newburgh Conspiracy to World War II, the effects of presidential illness on the decision to enter a war also becomes apparent. The mental and physical declines of Woodrow Wilson and Franklin Roosevelt had far-reaching effects after Versailles and Yalta. Conversely, Zachary Taylor's death helped to delay the onset of the Civil War, perhaps helping to ensure a Northern victory a decade later. The rise to power of Richard Olney after the demise of Walter Gresham, and Teddy Roosevelt upon the death of McKinley pushed the nation only deeper into imperialism.

Yet, the greatest change brought about by the various illnesses of the commanders-in-chief was the decline in the trust of the public toward government. Historians, political pundits, and sociologists have studied the phenomenon of declining public confidence in governance for decades. Most place the root of the movement in the late 1960s or early 1970s, blaming either the Vietnam War or Watergate for much of what the average citizen began to feel toward Washington. Once presidential disease and its associated medical cover-ups are analyzed, however, we can see that the roots of this distrust stretch back to the Gilded Age. Politicians, perhaps building on the case of William Crawford in 1824, have long sought to separate their health issues from political ones. With the amount of subterfuge employed by Grover Cleveland, Wilson, and FDR, it is not surprising that later generations of Americans might begin to become skeptical of the government.

Over the past two centuries, presidents or Congress attempted to address this issue. Presidential solutions ran from full disclosure and transparency to denials, cover-ups, reckless neglect of laws and amendments, or, as with Wilson and Dwight Eisenhower, transferal of power to others. For its part, Congress has attempted numerous times to pass laws and amendments in an effort to preserve the functions of government and ensure the will of the people, all of which culminated in the Twenty-fifth Amendment.

The people themselves, as the ultimate source of power for the government, have also become more vigilant in their concern over the health of their candidates. As early as 2013, both Republicans and the media were already beginning to question the age of presumed Democratic nominee Hillary Clinton if she ran for office in 2016. Her victory would make her as old as Reagan upon entering the White House, a man whose age was constantly brought up by Democrats both in 1980 and 1984.[321] Though some attempted to parlay the question into one of life expectancy, a number of health issues experienced by the then-secretary of state did little to soften the view of many.[322] In fact, a book published in 2014 detailed a cover-up by the perennial Democratic candidate and warned of an impending stroke.[323] Likewise, Clinton's own emails, released as part of the probe into her time at the State Department, reveal a woman who suffered blood clots, a transverse sinus thrombosis, a thyroid problem, cardiac stress, and double vision. A partial release from 2013 revealed that her top aide, Huma Abedin, cautioned an advisor to be sure to review details with Clinton because "She's often confused."[324] Perhaps one of the saving graces for her in the campaign though was the presence of an even older candidate, Sen. Bernie Sanders. Despite the fact that the age difference between the two was only six years, the noticeably older looking Sanders drew more questions about his health at debates than did Clinton. Both supporters and opponents of Clinton took to referring to Sanders by various age related nicknames including a "geriatric socialist."

As always though, the Founding Fathers did plan for such an occurrence, as the concept was certainly not lost upon them. The underlying foundation of all republics, ancient or modern, has always been the virtue of its citizens. Undoubtedly the two illnesses that caused the most damage to the nation were Wilson's and FDR's. Likewise, they were the two maladies most hidden from the public, both for less than honorable reasons. As Eisenhower and others have shown, an unhealthy but virtuous commander-in-chief was far superior to the public than one whose health was merely a façade. No doctor can ever prevent the illnesses of a president, and lives will be affected by and lost to disease well into the future. Yet, those running for office should not knowingly place the future of the nation in infirm or even dying hands. The public must press the issue with its candidates, and not gloss over important health concerns for the sake of a preferred candidate. Disease not only weakens individuals, but the handling of it, by revealing the character of the republic, can enervate or destroy the nation as well. As Hippocrates stated over 2,500 years ago, "It is more important to know what sort of person has a disease than to know what sort of disease a person has."

CHAPTER NOTES

Chapter 1

1 James Thomas Flexnor, *George Washington Vol. 3* (Boston: Little and Brown, 1965-1972), 6.

2 Letter, George Washington to John Augustine Washington (June 28, 1755)

3 Ibid. Doctor Robert James developed a fever powder in 1746 which consisted of chiefly phosphate of lime and oxide of antimony.

4 Letter, George Washington to Mary Ball Washington (July 18, 1755).

5 George Washington, *The Daily Journal of Maj. George Washington in 1751-1752* (Albany: Joel Munsell's Sons, 1892), 53.

6 See J.K. Kar et al., "Vaso-epididymal anastomosis," *Fertility and Sterility* No. 26 (1975) pp. 743-756, W.H. Ropper et al., "Primary Serofibrinous Pleural Effusion in Military Personnel," *American Review of Tuberculosis* No. 71 (1955) pp 616 –34, G.J. Gorse et al., "Male Genital Tuberculosis: A Review of the Literature with Instructive Case Reports", Review of Infectious Disease No. 7 (1985) pp 511–24, and W.I. Christensen, "Genitourinary Tuberculosis: Review of 102 Cases", *Medicine* No. 53 (1974) pp. 377–90.

7 Letter, James McHenry to George Washington (March 29, 1789).

8 Letter, Lewis Nicola to George Washington (May 22, 1782).

9 Letter, George Washington to Lewis Nicola (May 22, 1782).

10 Ron Chernow, "George Washington: The Reluctant President," *Smithsonian Magazine* (Feb. 2011).

11 Beginning with the Siege of Fort Pitt during Pontiac's Rebellion and continuing to the Evacuation of Boston in 1776, the British had attempted to employ smallpox while at war on numerous occasions.

12 Letter, Robert H. Harrison to Council of Massachusetts (December 3, 1775).

13 Letter, George Washington to President of Congress (December 19, 1775).

14 Letter, George Washington to Joseph Reed.

15 John E. Ferling. *The First of Men: A Life of George Washington* (New York: Oxford University Press, 2010), 139.

16 Letter, Archibald Cary to R. H. Lee (December 24, 1775).

17 Letter, George Washington to William Shippen (January 6, 1777).

18 David R. Petriello, *Bacteria and Bayonets: Disease in American Military History* (Philadelphia: Casemate, 2015), 68-75.
19 Michael Clodfelter, *Warfare and Armed Conflict: A Statistical Reference to Casualty and Other Figures, 1618-1991* (McFarland, 2002).
20 Johann David Schoepf, *Materia Medica Americana Potissimum Regni Vegetabilis* (Cincinnati, 1903).
21 George Washington as quoted by Shaul G. Massry et al. "History of Nephrology," *The American Journal of Nephrology* 1997:17:233-240.
22 Tilton.
23 See Petriello and Elizabeth A. Fenn, *Pox Americana* for a discussion of the role of disease in the Revolution.
24 As recalled by his aide Col. David Cobb.
25 Letter, George Washington to James McHenry (July 3, 1789).
26 Richard Swiderski, *Anthrax: A History* (McFarland, 2004), 7 and "The Papers of George Washington," University of Virginia, Number Five (Spring 2002). Though the exact diagnosis of anthrax is debated among historians and scientists.
27 Letter, James Madison to Edmund Randolph (June 24, 1789).
28 Letter, George Washington to Betty Washington Lewis (Oct. 12, 1789).
29 Ron Chernow, *Washington: A Life* (Penguin, 2010).
30 Jeanne Adams, *Revolutionary Medicine: The Founding Fathers and Mothers in Sickness and in Health* (NYU Press, 2013), 66.
31 Letter, George Washington to Henry Knox (Sept. 9, 1793).
32 Letter, George Washington to Lear (Sept. 10, 1793).
33 Carey, 32.
34 Letter, George Washington to Alexander Hamilton (Sept. 6, 1793).
35 See Martin Pernick's "Politics, Parties, and Pestilence: Epidemic Yellow Fever in Philadelphia and the Rise of the First Party System", for a statistical treatment of this idea.
36 Letter, George Washington to Alexander Spotswood (Sept. 14, 1798) and *The Diaries of George Washington, Vol. 6, 1 January 1790–13 December 1799*, ed. Donald Jackson and Dorothy Twohig (Charlottesville: University Press of Virginia, 1979), 313–314
37 Raymond Brighton, The Checkered Career of Tobias Lear (Portsmouth Marine Society, 1985)
38 Washington had previously been treated with mercury oxide for smallpox and malaria. These treatments possibly resulted in his loss of teeth, that would necessitate his famous dentures.
39 "Facts and Observations relative to the Disease of Cynanche Trachealis, or Croup" (abstract), *Philadelphia Medical and Physical Journal*, Dr. Elisha C. Dick's Letter to the Editor, dated October 7, 1808, Published May, 1809, p. 253 (supplement).
40 C. M. Harris, *The Papers of William Thornton Vol. I* (Charlottesville: University Press of Virginia, 1995), 528
41 Ibid.

Chapter 2

42 George Washington, "Farewell Address."

43 Letter, Samuel Smith to Thomas Jefferson (April 24, 1823).

44 Everett S. Brown, "The Presidential Election of 1824-1825," *Political Science Quarterly*, Vol. 40, No. 3 (Sept., 1925), 393.

45 Letter, James Madison to William H. Crawford (April 13, 1824).

46 Herbert L. Abrams, "Presidential Health and the Public Interest: The Campaign of 1992," *Political Psychology*, Vol. 16, No. 4 (Dec., 1995), 796.

47 Dumas Malone, *Jefferson and His Time Vol. VI: The Sage of Monticello* (Boston: Little Brown & Company, 1981), 432.

48 Letter, James Monroe to James Madison (Oct. 17, 1823).

49 Letter, John Quincy Adams to George Washington Adams (Oct. 21, 1823).

50 Letter, Thomas Jefferson to William H. Crawford (April 20, 1824).

51 Letter, Thomas Jefferson to Francis Walker Gilmer (Oct. 12, 1824).

52 He was 230 days older at the time of his inauguration than John Adams, who had previously held the record.

53 Benton Patterson, *The Generals: Andrew Jackson, Sir Edward Pakenham, and the Road to the Battle of New Orleans* (New York: NYU Press, 2005), 11.

54 This disease has been widely reported to have been cholera, yet major outbreaks would not occur in the West until almost forty years later. Dysentery or typhus are more likely to have been the cause of her death as it tended to be rampant on British prison ships during the war.

55 James Monroe as quoted in Michael P. Riccards, "The Presidency: In Sickness and Health," *Presidential Studies Quarterly*, Vol. 7, No. 4 (Fall 1977), 219.

56 Gretchen Vogel, "The Forgotten Malaria," *Science*, Vol. 342, No. 6159 (Nov. 2013), 684-687.

57 L.M. Deppisch et al., "Andrew Jackson's Exposure to Mercury and Lead: Poisoned President?", *JAMA*, 282(6) (1999), 569-571.

58 J.S. Bassett, *Correspondence of Andrew Jackson, Vol 1* (Washington, DC: Carnegie Institute of Washington, 1926), 439.

59 George Bancroft, *Memoirs of General Andrew Jackson* (Auburn NY: J.C. Derby, 1845), 37

60 Marquis James, *The Life of Andrew Jackson* (1938), as quoted in Rudolph Marx, *The Health of the Presidents* (New York: Putnam, 1960), 108-109.

61 Letter, Andrew Jackson to John Coffee (March 22, 1829).

62 Letter, Andrew Jackson to John Christmas McLemore (April 26, 1829).

63 Letter, Andrew Jackson to John Donelson (June, 7, 1829).

64 Fletcher M. Green, "On Tour with President Andrew Jackson," The New England Quarterly, Vol. 36, No. 2 (June 1963), 209.

65 George Green Shackelford, "From the Society's Collections: Lieutenant Lee Reports to Captain Talcott on Fort Calhoun's Construction on the Rip Raps," *The Virginia Magazine of History and Biography*, Vol. 60, No. 3 (July

1952), 467.

66 Letter, Andrew Jackson to James Alexander Hamilton (Sept. 11, 1829).

67 David Macaulay, "Civil War Anniversary Stirs Interest in Ft. Wool," *Daily Press*, (July 4, 2011).

68 William E. Smith, "Francis P. Blair, Pen-Executive of Andrew Jackson," *The Mississippi Valley Historical Review*, Vol. 17, No. 4 (March 1931), 554.

69 Green, 222

70 Jon Meacham, *American Lion: Andrew Jackson in the White House* (New York: Random House, 2010), 110.

71 Letter, Andrew Jackson to John Coffee (Sept. 21, 1829).

72 Ibid.

73 Marx, 114.

74 Green, 224.

75 Maureen T. Moore, "Andrew Jackson: 'Pretty near a 'Treason' to Call Him Doctor!'," *The New England Quarterly*, Vol. 62, No. 3 (Sept. 1989), 424-435.

76 Adams wrote that Jackson, "was so ravenous of notoriety that he craves sympathy for sickness...that is four-fifths trickery, and the other fifth mere fatigue." *Memoires of John Quincy Adams, Comprising Portions of his Diaries from 1795 to 1848*, Charles Francis Adams. ed. (Philadelphia: 1874-1877), IX, 4-5.

77 John C. Fitzpatrick, ed. *The Autobiography of Martin Van Buren* (US Printing Office, 1920), 326.

78 Fitzpatrick, 625.

79 Quoted in W.E. Beard, "The Autobiography of Martin Van Buren," *Tennessee Historical Magazine*, Vol. 6, No. 3 (Oct. 1920), 163.

80 Andrew Jackson, "1st State of the Union Address" (1829).

81 Letter, Henry Clay to Francis Preston Blair (January 29, 1825).

82 Arthur Meier Schlesinger, *The Imperial Presidency* (Houghton-Mifflin, 2004), 35.

83 Letter, Henry Clay to John B. Dillon (July 28, 1838).

84 *The Richmond Whig* (April 8, 1834).

85 Kenneth F. Kiple, ed., *Plague, Pox, & Pestilence* (New York: Barnes & Noble Books, 1997), 142.

86 Charles E. Rosenberg, *The Cholera Years: The United States in 1832, 1849, and 1866* (Chicago: The University of Chicago Press, 1962), 40.

87 Addison A. to Sanford Ferguson (July 18, 1832), Letter. *The Ferguson-Jayne Papers, 1826 - 1938*, Mary S. Briggs, ed., Interlaken New York: Heart of the Lakes Publishing, 1981.

88 Adam Jortner, "Cholera, Christ, and Jackson: The Epidemic of 1832 and the Origins of Christian Politics in Antebellum," *Journal of the Early Republic* (Summer 2007), 27

89 Catherine Drinker Bowen, *Yankee From Olympus: Justice Holmes and His Family* (Boston: Little Brown & Company, 1944), 69 and E. W. Stoughton, "The Third Term: Reasons For It," *The North American Review*, Vol. 130, No. 280 (March 1880), 229.

90 Benjamin Perley Poore, Perley's Reminiscences of Sixty Years in the Na-

tional Metropolis, Vol. 1 (London: 1886), 135

91 From the Herald as quoted in Timothy O. Howe, "The Third Term," The North American Review, Vol. 130, No. 279 (Feb. 1880), 127.

92 Dr. Fred Rodell, "Democracy and the Third Term: No. 6," *Pittsburgh Press*, (Aug. 23, 1940).

93 Andrew Jackson, Farewell Address (March 4, 1837).

94 Concerns over his frail health prompted the new president, Martin Van Buren, to order the surgeon general and several army doctors to accompany Jackson during his journey back to the Hermitage.

95 Deppisch et al., 569-571.

96 Marius is alleged by some ancient writers to have died from a lung infection or pleurisy, a similar ailment to Jackson's tuberculosis.

Chapter 3

97 See Madison's Notes for September 4 and September 7.

98 *Vermont Watchman and State Journal* (April 27, 1840).

99 See Ronald J. Zboray, "Gender Slurs in Boston's Partisan Press During the 1840s," *Journal of American Studies*, Vol. 34, No. 3 (Dec. 2000), 413-446.

100 Webster once famously quipped that in editing the speech he had, "killed seventeen Roman proconsuls." Quoted in Robert Remini, *Daniel Webster* (NY: 1997), 516.

101 *New York Tribune* (April 12, 1841).

102 Riccards, 220.

103 More recent medical opinion leans towards septicemia as the immediate cause of his death while older ones like Riccards suggest hepatitis.

104 *Edgefield Advertiser* (May 6, 1841), 1.

105 Letter, Henry Clay to John L. Lawrence (April 13, 1841).

106 Daniel Walker Howe, *What Hath God Wrought: The Transformation of America, 1815-1848* (Oxford University Press, 2007), 572.

107 *The Yazoo Whig* (April 30, 1841), 3.

108 Zachariah Frederick Smith, *The History of Kentucky: From its Earliest Discovery and Settlement to its Historic Characters* (Kentucky: Courier Company, 1892), 845.

109 Sunbury American Journal (July 29, 1843), 2.

110 Letter, Henry Clay to John M. Berrien (Sept. 4, 1843).

111 "The Last Hours of Ex-President Polk," *Sunbury American* (June 30, 1849), 2. The sealing of the bodies of those deceased from contagious disease inside metal coffins was a practice that continued well into the twentieth century. See *Bulletin of the National Research Council*, Issues 73-76 (National Academies, 1929), 134.

112 Lester Packer, *Vitamin C in Health and Disease* (New York: CRC Press, 1997), 15.

113 *New York Daily Tribune* (July 12, 1850), 4.

114 Daniel Webster to Hall (May 18, 1850).

115 "John C. Calhoun," *The Evansville Daily Journal* (March 7, 1850), 2.

116 H. Montgomery, *The Life of Major General Zachary Taylor* (1850), 425-426.

117 *Vermont Phoenix* (July 13, 1849), 2

118 See Millard Fillmore's speech in *Anti-slavery Bugle* (Dec. 7, 1850), 3

Chapter 4

119 James Madison's Notes on the Constitution (Sept. 7, 1787)

120 "At The Thousand Isles," The Sun (Oct. 1, 1882), 5.

121 *The True Northerner* (Oct. 13, 1882), 6.

122 Riccards, 223.

123 Thomas C. Reeves, "President Arthur in Yellowstone National Park," *Montana: The Magazine of Western History*, Vol. 19, No. 3 (Summer 1969), 18-29

124 "President Cleveland, Dr. Bryant, and Mr. Benedict Cruise," *The Indiana State Journal* (July 19, 1893), 1.

125 Allan Nevins, *The Letters of Grover Cleveland* (Houghton Mifflin, 1933), 530.

126 Robert H. Ferrell, *Ill-Advised: Presidential Health and Public-Trust* (University of Missouri Press, 1996), 6

127 Robert McNutt McElroy, *Grover Cleveland: The Man and Statesman* (Harper & Brothers, 1923), 30-31

128 "Simply a Tooth Pulled," *The Indiana State Journal* (Sept. 6, 1893), 1.

129 The truth of the story would not appear until twenty-four years later when Dr. Keen finally broke his silence about the entire operation. See Matthew Algeo's, *The President is a Sick Man* (Chicago: Chicago Review Press, 2011) for a complete treatment of the character assassination of Edwards by the White House.

130 Jean Edward Smith, *FDR* (Random House, 2007), 189.

131 Armond S. Goldman, et al., "What was the Cause of Franklin Delano Roosevelt's Paralytic Illness?" *Journal of Medical Biography* (2003), 232-240.

132 *The Brooklyn Daily Eagle* (Aug. 9, 1936), 55.

133 Naomi Rogers, *Dirt and Disease: Polio Before FDR* (Rutgers University Press, 1992), notes 232.

134 Earle Looker would go on to write a number of works on Theodore Roosevelt, Franklin Roosevelt, and Hoover including, *The White House Gang* (1929), *This Man Roosevelt* (1932), *Theodore Roosevelt: Private Citizen*(1932), and *The American Way: Franklin Roosevelt in Action* (1933).

135 *Liberty Magazine* (July 1931).

136 *Time* (Feb. 1, 1932).

137 See *Time* (Dec. 17, 1934) and *Life* (Jan. 20, 1941), among others.

138 *Editor & Publisher* (1936) as quoted in Matthew Pressman, "The Myth of FDR's Disability," *Time* (July 12, 2013).

139 Patricia Brennan, "A President Who Faced Fear Himself," *Washington Post* (April 17, 2005).

140 Riccards, 226.

141 As quoted in Joseph E. Persico, *Roosevelt's Secret War* (Random House: 2002),

277.

142 Harry S. Goldsmith, *A Conspiracy of Silence: The Health and Death of Franklin D. Roosevelt* (iUniverse: 2007), 193.

143 Letter, Dr. Frank Lahey (July 10, 1944).

144 Jerry N. Hess, "Oral History Interview With Robert G. Nixon" (Oct. 16, 1970) *Truman Library*, 98

145 Letter, J. Edgar Hoover to Stephen T. Early as quoted in H.S. Goldsmith, "Unanswered Mysteries in the Death of Franklin D. Roosevelt," *Surgery, Gynecology, & Obstetrics*, No. 149 (1979), 899-908.

146 Lahey.

147 Jack Anderson, "FDR Knew of Cancer Before his Last Term in Office," Kentucky New Era (July 2, 1987)

148 Hess, 76.

149 Patrick Hurley, *Atlantic Monthly* (Sept. 28, 1950).

150 Orville Dwyer Memo to editor of the *Chicago Tribune* (Jan. 5, 1948).

Chapter 5

151 John Milton Cooper, *Woodrow Wilson: A Biography* (Vintage Books, 2011), 109.

152 Ibid., 71.

153 Kenneth R. Crispell, *Hidden Illness in the White House* (Duke University Press, 1989), 25.

154 William g. Haynes, et al., "Periodontal Disease and Atherosclerosis: From Dental to Arterial Plaque," *Arteriosclerosis, Thrombosis, and Vascular Biology*, No. 23 (2003), 1309-1311.

155 Letter, Woodrow Wilson to Albert Bushnell Hart (Aug. 21, 1891).

156 Cooper, 71.

157 Edwin A. Weinstein, *Woodrow Wilson: A Medical and Physiological Biography* (Princeton University Press, 2014), 159-160.

158 Stockton Axson, *"Brother Woodrow": A Memoir of Woodrow Wilson* (Princeton University Press, 2014), 254.

159 Letter Cary T. Grayson to Alice Gertrude Gordon (Aug. 19, 1915).

160 "Wilson Pays Visit to Philadelphia," *NY Times* (Aug. 20, 1915).

161 Ferrell, 14 and Cooper, 201.

162 From Col. House's Diary as quoted in Cooper, 356.

163 Letter Cary T. Grayson to Alice Gertrude Gordon (July 16, 1918).

164 "Pres. Wilson Not Suffering From Influenza," *The Ogden Standard* (April 5, 1919), 1, "Diplomatic Aspect to Wilson's Illness Rumored," *El Paso Herald* (April 5, 1919),2 and "Conference Reports Material Progress," *The Washington Herald* (April 10, 1919), 2.

165 "President's Ship to Carry Dr. Da Costa to France," *Evening Public Ledger* (April 10, 1919), 1.

166 See John M. Barry's *The Great Influenza* for a deeper depiction of the effect

of the disease upon Wilson.

167 John M. Barry, *The Great Influenza: The Story of Deadliest Pandemic in History* (Penguin, 2005), 386.
168 Phyllis Lee Levin, *Edith and Woodrow: The Wilson White House*, 296.
169 Letter Cary T. Grayson to Samuel Ross (April 14, 1919).
170 Cooper, 525.
171 Letter, William H. Taft to A L Lowell (Oct. 5, 1919).
172 Ishbel Ross, *An American Family: The Tafts 1678-1904* (Cleveland: World Publishing Company, 1964), 316.
173 Hebert Hoover, *The Ordeal of Woodrow Wilson* (Woodrow Wilson Center Press, 1992), 275.
174 Ibid, 274.
175 Cooper, 552.
176 Edward B. MacMahon, *Medical Cover-ups in the White House* (Washington DC: Farragut, 1987), 75.
177 Letter, Carey T. Grayson to Carter Glass (June 16, 1920)
178 See Kurt Wimer, "Woodrow Wilson and a Third Nomination," *Pennsylvania History Journal*, Vol. 29, No. 2 (April 1962), 193-211 and Rixey Smith, *Carter Glass: A Biography* (Longmans, Green, and Company, 1939)

Chapter 6

179 *Memphis Daily Appeal* (May 13, 1881), 1.
180 "White House Malaria," *Memphis Daily Appeal* (May 13, 1881), 1.
181 John B. Roberts, *Rating the First Ladies: The Women Who Influenced the Presidency* (Citadel Press, 2004), 149.
182 *Omaha Daily Bee* (July 15, 1881), 1.
183 Willard Bliss, "Feeding Per Rectum: As Illustrated in the Case of the Late President Garfield and Others" *The Medical Record* (New York, 1882), 9.
184 "The Doctor's War," *Public Ledger* (Oct. 29, 1881), 4.
185 "Washington Letter," *The Arizona Sentinel* (April 22, 1882), 2.
186 James Rentfrow, *Home Squadron: The U.S. Navy on the North Atlantic Station* (Naval Institute Press, 2014), Chapter 2.
187 *The Evening World* (May 16, 1901), 1
188 *Evening Star* (Sept. 6, 1901), 5.
189 *The Wichita Daily Eagle* (Oct. 17, 1901), 4
190 "Unique Application for a Post Office," *The St. Louis Republic* (Feb. 22, 1901), 9
191 Francis Russell, *The Shadow of Blooming Grove: Warren G. Harding in His Times* (New York: McGraw-Hill, 1968), 331-332.
192 "Panama Canal is Inspected by Harding," *The Bismarck Tribune* (Nov. 24, 1920), 1.
193 Russell, 311.
194 Carl Sferrazza Anthony, "A President of the Peephole," *The Washington Post* (June 7, 1998).
195 John W. Dean, *Warren G. Harding* (New York: Macmillan, 2004), 147.

196 "Mrs. Harding Very Ill," *The Cook County News* (Sept. 14, 1922), 2.

197 Irwin Hood Hoover, 42 Years in the White House (Boston: Houghton and Mifflin Co., 1934), 268.

198 L.M. Deppisch, "Homeopathic medicine and presidential health: homeopathic influences upon two Ohio presidents," *Pharos*, Vol. 60 (Fall 1997), 5-10.

199 "Harding's Illness Ends Week's Engagements," NY Times (Jan. 19, 1923), 1.

Chapter 7

200 Stephen E. Ambrose, *Eisenhower: Soldier and President* (Simon and Schuster, 2014), 299.

201 As quoted in Robert Watson et al., "Reconsidering Ike's Health and Legacy: A Surprising Lesson in Duty at the Little White House Residential Retreat," Eisenhower Institute.

202 "Truman Doubts Eisenhower Will Make Presidential Bid," *Reading Eagle* (Dec. 23, 1949), 10.

203 Steffan Andrews, "Will Ellis Arnall Resign," *The Spokesman Review* (May 12, 1952), 4.

204 "Taft's Cancer Originated in Pancreas, Doctor Says," Chicago Tribune (Oct. 3, 1953), 7.

205 Robert E. Gilbert, *The Mortal Presidency: Illness and Anguish in the White House* (Fordham Press, 1998), 89.

206 "Good Behavior Wins President Sixth Star," *St. Petersburg Times* (Oct. 23, 1955), 1.

207 *St. Petersburg Times* (Oct. 23, 1955), 1.

208 Richard Nixon, *Six Crises* (New York: Doudleday, 1962), 138.

209 "Republican's Election Dilemma," *The Glasgow Herald* (Dec. 13, 1955), 7.

210 "Sir Winnie Admits Grave 1953 Illness," *The Victoria Advocate* (March 3, 1955), 9.

211 David Sentner, "Churchill's Illness Got Eisenhower Off Hook," *The Milwaukee Sentinel* (June 29, 1953), 5.

212 Richard Nixon, *In the Arena* (New York: Simon and Schuster, 1990).

213 Ibid.

214 Gilbert, 95.

215 David Lawrence, "Questions about Eisenhower's Future," *Sarasota Herald-Tribune* (Oct. 16, 1955), 4.

216 Nixon would have just turned forty-three at the time of his inauguration, making him the youngest elected president. Jim Newton, Eisenhower: The White House Years (Knopf Doubleday, 2012), 203.

217 Joe Belden, "The Texas Poll," *The Victoria Advocate* (Jan. 2, 1956), 4.

218 Gilbert, 99.

219 Ibid., 101.

220 "The World Today," *The Virgin Islands Daily News* (Nov. 17, 1955), 1.

221 Gilbert, 104.

222 "Eisenhower's Illness Called a Little Stroke," *NY Times* (Nov. 27, 1957).

223 "Without 25th Amendment Albert and Democrats Would be in the White House," *Gettysburg Times* (Dec. 21, 1974), 9.

224 These include the Presidential Succession Acts of 1792, 1886, and 1947.

225 "25th Amendment's Repeal Said Likely," *Sarasota Journal* (Sept. 25, 1974).

226 "Reagan Vows to Resign if Doctors in White House Finds him Unfit," *NY Times* (June 11, 1980).

227 As Quoted in Herbert L. Adams, *The President Has Been Shot: Confusion, Disability, and the 25th Amendment* (Stanford University Press, 1994), 72.

228 Richard V. Allen, "When Reagan was shot, who was 'in control' at the White House?", *Washington Post* (March 23, 2011).

229 Ronald Reagan, letter to Tip O'Neill (July 13, 1985).

230 Ronald Reagan, letter to America (November 5, 1994).

Chapter 8

231 Thomas H. Maugh, "John F. Kennedy's Addison's disease was probably caused by rare autoimmune disease," *LA Times* (Sept. 5, 2009).

232 Robert Dallek, *An Unfinished Life: John F. Kennedy 1917-1963* (Boston: Little, Brown, 2003), 103.

233 Ibid., 123.

234 Michael O'Brien, *John F. Kennedy: A Biography* (New York: Macmillan, 2006), 160-161.

235 Ibid., 760 note.

236 Robert Dallek, "The Medical Ordeals of JFK," *The Atlantic* (Dec. 2002) and L.R. Mandel LR, "Endocrine and Autoimmune Aspects of the Health History of John F. Kennedy," *Annals of Internal Medicine*, 151 (2009) 350-354.

237 Eleanor Roosevelt, "On My Own," *Saturday Evening Post* (March 8, 1958).

238 Walter Trohan, "Jack Once Donated to Help Nixon," *The Miami News* (July 25, 1960), 22.

239 Sally Bedell Smith, *Grace and Power: The Private World of the Kennedy White House* (Random House Publishing, 2006), 33.

240 Gilbert, 157.

241 Dallek, "The Medical Ordeals of JFK."

242 Peter Keating, "The Strange Saga of JFK and the Original 'Dr. Feelgood'," *NY Magazine* (Nov. 22, 2013).

243 Jerrold M. Post, *When Illness Strikes the Leader: The Dilemma of the Captive King* (New Have: Yale University Press, 1993), 69-70.

244 Keating.

245 John Nichols, "President Kennedy's Adrenals," *Journal of the American Medical Association* (1967).

Chapter 9

246 Letter, John McKinley to James Madison (June 1, 1812).

247 Letter, Henry Dearborn to Thomas Jefferson (March 10, 1812).

248 Letter, Dolley Madison to Anna Payne Cutts (March 27, 1812).

249 James K. Polk, *The Diary of James K. Polk Vol. 3* (Chicago: A.C. McClurg and Co., 1910), 419.

250 Louise Mayo, *James K. Polk: The Dark Horse President* (Nova Publishers, 2006), 138.

251 James K. Polk, The Diary of James K. Polk Vol. 4(Chicago: A.C. McClurg and Co., 1910), 412.

252 Mark E. Byrnes, James K. Polk: A Biographical Companion (ABC-CLIO, 2001), 51.

253 Ruth T. Feldman, *Chester A. Arthur* (Twenty First Century Books, 2006), 85.

254 See Schrank's letters in Oliver Remy's, *The Attempted Assassination of ex-President Theodore Roosevelt* (Milwaukee: Progressive Publishing Association, 1912).

255 Russell, 311.

256 See Don Hewitt's *Tell Me a Story: Fifty Years and 60 Minutes in Television* (Public Affairs, 2002) for a good discussion of the debate.

257 James R. Jones, "Behind LBJ's Decision Not to Run in '68," NY Times (April 16, 1988).

258 Richard Novak who broke the story and the quote in 1972 revealed his source years later to be Sen. Thomas Eagleton, McGovern's future running mate.

259 Joshua M. Glasser, *Eighteen Day Running Mate: McGovern. Eagleton, and a Campaign in Crisis* (Yale University Press, 2012), 149-150.

260 Joe Garofoli, "Obama Bounces Back- Speech Seemed to Help," *San Francisco Gate* (March 26, 2008).

261 David Lauter, "Reagan Remark Spurs Dukakis Health Report," *LA Times* (Aug. 4, 1988).

262 Michael Wines, "Bush in Japan," *NY Times* (Jan. 9, 1992).

263 Sidney Blumenthal, "Atwater's Legacy," *The New Yorker* (Oct. 19, 1992).

264 Richard L. Berke, "Still Running; Is Age Bashing the Way to Beat Bob Dole?" *NY Times* (May 5, 1996).

265 "The Second Clinton-Dole Presidential Debate," (Oct. 16, 1996).

266 Ibid.

267 Alan Silverleib, "Analysis: Age an issue in the 2008 campaign?" *CNN* (June 15, 2008)

268 Andrew Malcolm, "Oops, Obama ad mocks McCain's inability to send e-mail. Trouble is, he can't due to tortured fingers," *LA Times* (Sept. 13, 2008)

269 Lawrence Altman, "On the Campaign Trail, Few Mentions of McCain's Bout with Melanoma," *NY Times* (March 9, 2008).

Chapter 10

270 James Trecothick Austin, *The Life of Elbridge Gerry*, Vol. 2 (Wells and Lily, 1829), 399-400.
271 Ludwig M. Deppisch, *The White House Physician: A History from Washington to George Bush* (McFarland, 2007), 186.
272 John Hoyt Williams, *Sam Houston* (Simon and Schuster, 1994), 61.
273 Daniel Fate Brooks, "William Rufus King," in L. Edward Purcell ed., *Vice Presidents: A Biographical Dictionary* (Infobase Publishing, 2010), 134.
274 Elias Nason, *The Life and Public Services of Henry Wilson* (B.B. Russell, 1876), 419.
275 Ibid., 423.
276 Ibid., 426.
277 *Memorial Addresses on the Life and Character of Thomas A. Hendricks* (US Congress, 49th Congress, 1st Session, 1886), 27-28.
278 Andrew E. Stoner, *Wicked Indianapolis* (The History Press, 2011), 99.
279 Letter, William McKinley to Garret Hobart (Sept. 2, 1899).
280 Michael J. Connolly, "'I Make Politics my Recreation': Vice President Garret Hobart and Nineteenth-Century Republican Business Politics, *New Jersey History* 125:1, 39.

Chapter 11

281 Helen Bryan, *Martha Washington: First Lady of Liberty* (Wiley, 2007), 205-206.
282 Willard Sterne Randall, Thomas Jefferson: A Life (New York: Harper Perennial, 1994), 347.
283 Letter, Dolley Madison to Mary Latrobe (Dec. 3, 1814).
284 August C. Buell, *History of Andrew Jackson Vol. II* (New York, 1904), 204.
285 Phyllis Lee Levin, *Abigail Adams: A Biography* (Macmillan, 2001), 455.
286 Diary Entry of Louisa Catherine Adams (Nov. 18, 1801) in *Louisa Catherine Adams, A Traveled First Lady* (Harvard University Press, 2014).
287 Lewis L. Gould, *American First Ladies: Their Lives and Their Legacy* (Routledge, 2014), 51.
288 Deppisch, 34.
289 Letter, Abigail Fillmore to Mary Abigail Fillmore (July 1844) Quoted in Robert J. Scarry, *Millard Fillmore* (McFarland, 2001), 126.
290 Molly Meijer Wertheimer, ed., *Inventing a Voice: The Rhetoric of American First Ladies of the 20th Century* (Rowman & Littlefield Publishers, 2004), 35.
291 Bill Harris, *The First Ladies Fact Book* (Black Dog & Leventhal, 2012), 352.
292 Ibid., 353.
293 Gould, 242.

Chapter 12

294 *Harper's Young People: 1881*, Vol. 2 (Harper and Brothers, 1881), 259-260.
295 Letter, Benjamin Rush to Abigail Adams Smith (August 1811).
296 Letter, John Adams to Thomas Jefferson (August 10, 1813).
297 Letter Thomas Jefferson to John Adams (October 12, 1813).
298 Letter, Abigail Adams to Mary Smith Cranch (December 1800).
299 Ibid.
300 Letter, James Currie to Thomas Jefferson (Nov. 20, 1784).
301 Letter, Ellen Wayles Randolph Coolidge to Henry S. Randall (Jan. 15, 1856).
302 Letter, Abigail Adams to Thomas Jefferson (May 20, 1804).
303 Letter, Thomas Jefferson to Abigail Adams (June 13, 1804).
304 Robert W. Ikard, "Surgical Operation on James K. Polk by Ephraim McDowell or the Search for Polk's Gallstone," *Tennessee Historical Quarterly*, Vol. 43, No. 2 (Summer 1984), 121-131.
305 Letter, James Fenimore Cooper to William Gore Ouseley (July 23, 1832).
306 Letter, Jane Pierce to Mary Aiken (1836).
307 John Sotos, *The Physical Lincoln* (Mt. Vernon Books, 2008).
308 "Death of 'Tad' Lincoln," *Belmont Chronicle* (July 20, 1871), 2.
309 "Robbing the Grave," *The Daily Cairo Bulletin* (June 1, 1878), 2.
310 Letter, Theodore Roosevelt to John Burroughs (Aug. 14, 1918).
311 Dan P. McAdams, George W. Bush and the Redemptive Dream (New York: Oxford University Press, 2010), 12.
312 "Secretary Gresham Dead," *Salt Lake City Herald* (May 28, 1895), 1.
313 Letter, Richard Olney to Lord Salisbury (1895) in Willard Leon Beaulac, *The Fractured Continent: Latin America in Close-up* (Hoover Press), 57.

Chapter 13

314 Cotton Mather, *Diary* (May 26, 1721).
315 Cotton Mather, *Diary* (July 16, 1721).
316 Avik Roy, "A History Seminar: Obamacare Has Nothing to Do with Seamen Mandate of 1798," *Forbes* (Feb. 6, 2011).
317 Upton Sinclair, *The Jungle*.
318 Ibid.
319 "Report on Findings from the U.S. Public Health Service Sexually Transmitted Disease Inoculation Study of 1946–1948, Based on Review of Archived Papers of John Cutler, MD, at the University of Pittsburgh," (Dept. of Health and Human Services)
320 Robert Kennedy, "Deadly Immunity," *Rolling Stone* (June 20, 2005).

Conclusion

321 Jonathan Martin, "Republicans Paint Clinton as Old News for 2016 Presidential Election," *NY Times* (June 29, 2013).

322 Stephanie Stamm, "Why You Can't Compare Hillary Clinton's Age to Ronald Reagan's," *National Journal* (April 23, 2014).

323 Edward Klein, *Blood Feud* (Regnery Publishing, 2014).

324 Email, Huma Abedin to Monica Hanley (Jan. 26, 2013) US Dept. of State, Case No. F-2015-06322, Doc. No. C05836665 (Oct. 30, 2015).

SELECT BIBLIOGRAPHY

Abrams, Herbert L. "Presidential Health and the Public Interest: The Campaign of 1992," *Political Psychology*, Vol. 16, No. 4 (Dec., 1995).

Adams, Charles Francis, ed., *Memoirs of John Quincy Adams, Comprising Portions of his Diaries from 1795 to 1848*. Philadelphia: 1874-1877

Adams, Herbert L. *The President Has Been Shot: Confusion, Disability, and the 25th Amendment*. Stanford: Stanford University Press, 1994

Adams, Jeanne. *Revolutionary Medicine: The Founding Fathers and Mothers in Sickness and in Health*. New York: NYU Press, 2013

Algeo, Matthew. *The President is a Sick Man*. Chicago: Chicago Review Press, 2011

Ambrose, Stephen. *Eisenhower: Soldier and President*. New York: Simon and Schuster, 2014

Austin, James Trecothick. *The Life of Elbridge Gerry*, Vol. 2. New York: Wells and Lily, 1829

Axson, Stockton. *"Brother Woodrow": A Memoir of Woodrow Wilson*. Princeton University Press, 2014

Bancroft, George. *Memoirs of General Andrew Jackson*. Auburn NY: J.C. Derby, 1845

Barry, John M. *The Great Influenza: The Story of Deadliest Pandemic in History*. New York: Penguin, 2005

Bassett, J.S. *Correspondence of Andrew Jackson*. Vol 1. Washington, DC: Carnegie Institute of Washington, 1926

Beard, W.E. "The Autobiography of Martin Van Buren," *Tennessee Historical Magazine*, Vol. 6, No. 3 (Oct. 1920), 145-165.

Bliss, Willard. "Feeding Per Rectum: As Illustrated in the Case of the Late President Garfield and Others" *The Medical Record*. New York, 1882.

Bowen, Catherine Drinker. *Yankee From Olympus: Justice Holmes and His Family*. Boston: Little Brown & Company, 1944

Briggs, Mary S. *The Ferguson-Jayne Papers, 1826-1938*. Interlaken New York: Heart of the Lakes Publishing, 1981

Brighton, Raymond. *The Checkered Career of Tobias Lear*. Portsmouth Marine Society, 1985

Brown, Everett S. "The Presidential Election of 1824-1825,"*Political Science Quarterly*, Vol. 40, No. 3 (Sep., 1925).

Bryan, Helen. *Martha Washington: First Lady of Liberty*. New York: Wiley, 2007

Buell, August C. *History of Andrew Jackson* Vol. II. New York, 1904

Byrnes, Mark E. *James K. Polk: A Biographical Companion*. ABC-CLIO, 2001

Chernow, Ron. "George Washington: The Reluctant President," *Smithsonian Magazine* (Feb. 2011)

Christensen, W.I. "Genitourinary Tuberculosis: Review of 102 Cases," *Medicine* No. 53 (1974), 377–90.

Clodfelter, Michael. *Warfare and Armed Conflict: A Statistical Reference to Casualty and Other Figures, 1618-1991*. New York: McFarland, 2002

Connolly, Michael J. "I Make Politics my Recreation: Vice President Garret Hobart and Nineteenth-Century Republican Business Politics", *New Jersey History* 125:1.

Cooper, John Milton. *Woodrow Wilson: A Biography*. New York: Vintage Books, 2011

Crispell, Kenneth. *Hidden Illness in the White House*. Durham: Duke University Press, 1989

Dallek, Robert. *An Unfinished Life: John F. Kennedy 1917-1963*. Boston: Little, Brown, 2003

Dean, John W. *Warren G. Harding*. New York: Macmillan, 2004

Deppisch, L.M. et al., "Andrew Jackson's Exposure to Mercury and Lead: Poisoned President?", *JAMA*, 282(6) (1999), 569-571.

Deppisch, L.M. "Homeopathic medicine and presidential health: homeopathic influences upon two Ohio presidents," *Pharos* Vol. 60 (Fall 1997), 5-10.

Deppisch, Ludwig M. *The White House Physician: A History from Washington to George Bush*. New York: McFarland, 2007

Feldman, Ruth T. *Chester A. Arthur*. New York: Twenty First Century Books, 2006

Ferling, John E. *The First of Men: A Life of George Washington*. New York: Oxford University Press, 2010

Ferrell, Robert H. *Ill-Advised: Presidential Health and Public-Trust*. St. Louis: University of Missouri Press, 1996

Fitzpatrick, John C., ed. *The Autobiography of Martin Van Buren*. US Printing Office, 1920

Flexnor, James Thomas. *George Washington*, Vol. 3. Boston: Little and Brown, 1965-1972

Gilbert, Robert E. *The Mortal Presidency: Illness and Anguish in the White House*. Fordham Press, 1998

Glasser, Joshua M. *Eighteen Day Running Mate: McGovern. Eagleton, and a Campaign in Crisis*. New Haven: Yale University Press, 2012

Goldman, Armond S. et al., "What was the Cause of Franklin Delano Roosevelt's Paralytic Illness?" *Journal of Medical Biography* (2003), 232-240.

Goldsmith, Harry S. *A Conspiracy of Silence: The Health and Death of Franklin D. Roosevelt*. iUniverse: 2007

Gorse, G.J. et al. "Male Genital Tuberculosis: A Review of the Literature with Instructive Case Reports", *Review of Infectious Disease* No. 7 (1985), 511–24.

Gould, Lewis L. *American First Ladies: Their Lives and Their Legacy*. New York: Routledge, 2014

Green, Fletcher M. "On Tour with President Andrew Jackson," *The New England Quarterly*, Vol. 36, No. 2 (June 1963), 209-228.

Harris, Bill *The First Ladies Fact Book*. New York: Black Dog Publishing, 2009

Harris, C.M. *The Papers of William Thornton* Vol. I. Charlottesville: University Press of Virginia, 1995

Haynes, William G., et al. "Periodontal Disease and Atherosclerosis: From Dental to Arterial Plaque," *Arteriosclerosis, Thrombosis, and Vascular Biology* No. 23 (2003), 1309-1311.

Hogan, Margaret. *Louisa Catherine Adams: A Traveled First Lady*. Boston: Harvard University Press, 2014

Hoover, Herbert. *The Ordeal of Woodrow Wilson*. Washington, DC: Woodrow Wilson Center Press, 1992

Hoover, Irwin Hood. *42 Years in the White House*. Boston: Houghton and Mifflin Co., 1934

Howe, Daniel Walker. *What Hath God Wrought: The Transformation of America, 1815-1848*. Oxford University Press, 2007

Howe, Timothy O. "The Third Term," *The North American Review*, Vol. 130, No. 279 (Feb. 1880), 116-129.

Ikard, Rober W. "Surgical Operation on James K. Polk by Ephraim Mc-Dowell or the Search for Polk's Gallstone," *Tennessee Historical Quarterly*, Vol. 43, No. 2 (Summer 1984), 121-131.

Jortner, Adam. "Cholera, Christ, and Jackson: The Epidemic of 1832 and the Origins of Christian Politics in Antebellum." *Journal of the Early Republic* (Summer 2007)

Kar, J.K., et al., "Vaso-epididymal anastomosis", *Fertility and Sterility* No. 26 (1975), 743-756.

Kiple, Kenneth F., ed. *Plague, Pox, & Pestilence*. New York: Barnes & Noble Books, 1997

Klein, Edward. *Blood Feud*. Washington: Regnery Publishing, 2014

Levin, Phyllis Lee. *Edith and Woodrow: The Wilson White House*. New York: Scribner, 2001.

Levin, Phyllis Lee. *Abigail Adams: A Biography*. New York: Macmillan, 2001

MacMahon, Edward B. *Medical Cover-ups in the White House*. Washington DC: Farragut, 1987

Malone, Dumas. *Jefferson and His Time* Vol. VI: The Sage of Monticello. Boston: Little Brown & Company, 1981

Mandel, L.R., "Endocrine and Autoimmune Aspects of the Health History of John F. Kennedy," *Annals of Internal Medicine*, 151 (2009) 350-354.

Massry, Shaul G., et al., "History of Nephrology", *The American Journal of Nephrology*, 17 (1997), 233-240.

Mayo, Louise. *James K. Polk: The Dark Horse President*. New York: Nova Publishers, 2006

McAdams, Dan P. *George W. Bush and the Redemptive Dream*. New York: Oxford University Press, 2010

McElroy, Robert McNutt. *Grover Cleveland: The Man and Statesman*. New York: Harper & Brothers, 1923

Meacham, Jon. *American Lion: Andrew Jackson in the White House*. New York: Random House, 2010

Montgomery, H. *The Life of Major General Zachary Taylor*. 1850

Moore, Maureen T. "Andrew Jackson: 'Pretty near a 'Treason' to Call Him Doctor!,'" *The New England Quarterly*, Vol. 62, No. 3 (Sept. 1989), 424-435.

Nason, Elias. *The Life and Public Services of Henry Wilson*. B.B. Russell, 1876

Nevins, Allan. *The Letters of Grover Cleveland*. New York: Houghton Mifflin, 1933

Newton, Jim. *Eisenhower: The White House Years*. New York: Knopf Doubleday, 2012

Nichols, John. "President Kennedy's Adrenals," *JAMA* (1967)

Nixon, Richard. *Six Crises*. New York: Doubleday, 1962

Nixon, Richard. *In the Arena*. New York: Simon and Schuster, 1990.

O'Brien, Michael. *John F. Kennedy: A Biography*. New York: Macmillan, 2006

Packer, Lester. *Vitamin C in Health and Disease*. New York: CRC Press, 1997

Patterson, Benton. *The Generals: Andrew Jackson, Sir Edward Pakenham, and the Road to the Battle of New Orleans*. New York: NYU Press, 2005

Persico, Joseph E. *Roosevelt's Secret War*. New York: Random House: 2002

Petriello, David R. *Bacteria and Bayonets: Disease in American Military History*. Philadelphia: Casemate, 2016

Polk, James K. *The Diary of James K. Polk* Vol. 3-4. Chicago: A.C. McClurg and Co., 1910

Poore, Benjamin Perley. *Perley's Reminiscences of Sixty Years in the National Metropolis* Vol. 1. London: 1886

Post, Jerrold M. *When Illness Strikes the Leader: The Dilemma of the Captive King*. New Haven: Yale University Press, 1993

Randall, Willard Sterne. *Thomas Jefferson: A Life*. New York: Harper Perennial, 1994

Reeves, Thomas C. "President Arthur in Yellowstone National Park," *Montana: The Magazine of Western History*, Vol. 19, No. 3 (Summer 1969), 18-29.

Remy, Oliver. *The Attempted Assassination of ex-President Theodore Roosevelt*. Milwaukee: Progressive Publishing Association, 1912

Rentfrow, James. *Home Squadron: The U.S. Navy on the North Atlantic Station*. Annapolis: Naval Institute Press, 2014

Riccards, Michael P. "The Presidency: In Sickness and Health," *Presidential Studies Quarterly*, Vol. 7, No. 4 (Fall 1977), 215-231.

Roberts, John B. *Rating the First Ladies: The Women Who Influenced the Presidency*. New York: Citadel Press, 2004

Rogers, Naomi. *Dirt and Disease: Polio Before FDR*. New Brunswick: Rutgers University Press, 1992

Ropper, W.H. et al., "Primary Serofibrinous Pleural Effusion in Military Personnel," *American Review of Tuberculosis* No. 71 (1955), 616 –34.

Rosenberg, Charles E. *The Cholera Years: The United States in 1832, 1849, and 1866*. Chicago: The University of Chicago Press, 1962

Ross, Ishbel. *An American Family: The Tafts 1678-1904*. Cleveland: World Publishing Company, 1964

Russell, Francis. *The Shadow of Blooming Grove: Warren G. Harding in His Times*. New York: McGraw-Hill, 1968

Scarry, Robert J. *Millard Fillmore*. New York: McFarland, 2001

Schlesinger, Arthur M. *The Imperial Presidency*. New York: Houghton-Mifflin, 2004

Schoepf, Johann David. *Materia Medica Americana Potissimum Regni Vegetabilis*. Cincinnati, 1903

Shackelford, George Green. "From the Society's Collections: Lieutenant Lee Reports to Captain Talcott on Fort Calhoun's Construction on the Rip Raps," *The Virginia Magazine of History and Biography*, Vol. 60, No. 3 (July 1952), 458-487.

Smith, Jean Edward. *FDR*. New York: Random House, 2007

Smith, Rixey. *Carter Glass: A Biography*. New York: Longmans, Green, and Company, 1939

Smith, Sally Bedell. *Grace and Power: The Private World of the Kennedy White House*. New York: Random House Publishing, 2006

Smith, William E. "Francis P. Blair, Pen-Executive of Andrew Jackson," *The Mississippi Valley Historical Review*, Vol. 17, No. 4 (March 1931), 543-556.

Smith, Zachariah Frederick. *The History of Kentucky: From its Earliest Discovery and Settlement to its Historic Characters*. Kentucky: Courier Company, 1892

Sotos, John. *The Physical Lincoln*. Richmond: Mt. Vernon Books, 2008

Stoner, Andrew E. *Wicked Indianapolis*. Charleston: The History Press, 2011

Stoughton, E.W. "The Third Term: Reasons For It," *The North American Review*, Vol. 130, No. 280 (March 1880), 224-235.

Swiderski, Richard. *Anthrax: A History*. New York: McFarland, 2004

Vogel, Gretchen. "The Forgotten Malaria," *Science*, Vol. 342, No. 6159, (Nov. 2013), 684-687.

Washington, George. *The Daily Journal of Maj. George Washington in 1751-1752*. Albany: Joel Munsell's Sons, 1892.

Watson, Robert et al.. "Reconsidering Ike's Health and Legacy: A Surprising Lesson in Duty at the Little White House Residential Retreat," Gettysburg: The Eisenhower Institute at Gettysburg College.

Weinstein, Edwin A. *Woodrow Wilson: A Medical and Physiological Biography*. Princeton University Press, 2014

Wertheimer, Molly Meijer. *Inventing a Voice: The Rhetoric of American First Ladies of the 20th Century*. New York: Rowman, 2004.

Williams, John Hoyt. *Sam Houston*. New York: Simon and Schuster, 1994

Wimer, Kurt. "Woodrow Wilson and a Third Nomination," Pennsylvania *History Journal* Vol. 29, No. 2 (April 1962), 193-211.

Zboray, Ronald J. "Gender Slurs in Boston's Partisan Press During the 1840s," *Journal of American Studies*, Vol. 34, No. 3 (Dec. 2000), 413-446.

INDEX

and healthcare reform, 159
Clinton, George, 119
  election of 1812, 104
Clinton, Hillary, 164-165
Compromise of 1850, 36-38
Crawford, William H., 18-19
Crohn's Disease, 80, 85
Diphtheria, 2, 156
Disease(s)
  see individual disease entries
Dole, Robert, 116
Douglas, Stephen, 38
Dukakis, Michael, 113
Dunmore, Lord, 6
Dysentery, 2, 10, 38, 44, 131
Eagleton, Thomas, 113
Eaton Affair, 24
Eisenhower, Dwight D., 79-89
  and Crohn's Disease, 80
  and heart disease, 80-81, 85
  public announcement on health, 82
  effect on the Geneva Summit, 83
  the election of 1956, 85-86
  secret letter to Nixon on health, 87
  election of 1960, 111
  healthcare reform, 159
Elections
  see individual presidents
Epidemics
  see individual diseases
Fillmore, Abigail, 132
Fillmore, Millard, 38, 143-144
Ford, Gerald, 90
French and Indian War, 2, 7
Gallbladder, 88
Garfield, James A., 67-69
  treatment of, 68-69
  effects of death, 69-70
Garfield, Lucretia R., 68
Gerry, Elbridge, 120
Grant, Ulysses S., 106-107
Grayson, Cary, 59, 62-63
Great Yellow Fever Epidemic, 11-14, 25
  and the US government, 12-13

Greeley, Horace, 106-108
  death of wife, 107
  death of, 108
Gresham, Walter, 149-150
Guiteau, Charles, 67-69
Haig, Alexander, 93-94
Haitian Revolution, 12
Hamilton, Alexander, 12-14,
Harding, Warren G., 75-78
  compared to FDR's health, 47
  election of 1920, 75
  death of, 77-78
  conspiracies surrounding death, 78
Harrison, Benjamin, 147
Harrison, Caroline, 133
Harrison, William Henry, 31, 79
  age as an issue, 32
  treatment of, 32
Heart Disease, 49, 57, 69, 77, 80, 104, 112, 124, 130
Hemings, Sally, 128
Hemorrhoids, 2
Hendricks, Thomas, 123
Hepatitis, 32
Hobart, Garret, 124-125
Hopkins, Harry, 50
Humphrey, Hubert, 88
  and Eisenhower's health, 80
Hunt, William, 69-70
Huntington, Samuel, 30
Hutchinson, James, 12-13
Immigration and disease, 143-144
Influenza, 11, 34-35, 77
  Tehran Flu, 50
  Spanish Influenza, 61-63; *also see* Tyler, John and Washington, George
Inoculation, 4-7, 126, 161
  George Washington and, 7
Jackson, Andrew, 19-29
  election of 1824, 19
  election of 1828, 20
  early life, 20
  invasion of Florida, 21
  duels, 21-22

ABOUT THE AUTHOR

DAVID R. PETRIELLO was born in 1980 in Montclair, New Jersey. He completed his B.A. in Asian Studies at Seton Hall University before going on to receive an M.A. in History from Montclair State University and a Ph.D. in History from St. John's University. Previous books include *American Prometheus: Ronald Reagan and the Modernization of China*, *The Military History of New Jersey*, *Bacteria and Bayonets: The Impact of Disease on American Military History*, *The Days of Heroes Are Over: A Brief Biography of Richard Mentor Johnson*, and *The Dragon at War: A General Military History of China*. He currently teaches at Caldwell University in New Jersey.

www.ingramcontent.com/pod-product-compliance
Lightning Source LLC
Chambersburg PA
CBHW021400090426
42742CB00009B/941